BLOODY OCTOBER IN MOSCOW

BLOODY OCTOBER IN MOSCOW

Political Repression in the Name of Reform

by Alexander Buzgalin
and Andrei Kolganov

Translated by Renfrey Clarke

Monthly Review Press
New York

Copyright © 1994 by Monthly Review Press
All rights reserved

Library of Congress Cataloging-in-Publication Data
Buzgalin, A.V. (Alexander Vladimirovich)
  Bloody October in Moscow: Political repression in the name
of reform / by Alexander Buzgalin and Andrei Kolganov ; translated by
Renfrey Clarke.
   p. cm.
   ISBN 0–85345–895–2 : $26.00 — ISMB 0–85345–896–0 (pbk.) :
$15.00
   1. Russia (Federation)—Politics and government—1991– 2. Russia
(Federation). S"ezd narodnykh deputatov. 3. Yeltsin, Boris Nikolayevich,
1931– . I. Kolganov, A.I. (Andrei Ivanovich) II. Clarke, Renfrey. III. Title.
DK510.763.B89   1994
947.086—dc20   94–11816
                                                 CIP

Monthly Review Press
122 West 27th Street
New York, NY 10001

Manufactured in the United States of America
10 9 8 6 5 4 3 2 1

CONTENTS

FOREWORD 7

1. PRELUDE 9

2. CONFLICT 33

3. BLOOD 79

4. AFTERMATH 163

5. THE POST-OCTOBER REGIME 195

NEWSPAPERS CITED 213

FOREWORD

Work on this book began immediately after the bloody events of October 1993 in Moscow. At first we confined ourselves to collecting testimonies from eyewitnesses, but later we realized the need to provide a more thorough interpretation of everything that had occurred. We began expanding the manuscript to include an analysis of the causes of the conflict, its evolution, and its consequences. Where we did not ourselves have factual materials, we used press reports. We also included a number of documents that were important for providing a more exact understanding of events.

In selecting press articles or excerpts from them, we aimed to bring to light those aspects of the events that were ignored by the semi-official mass media. The version favored by the people who prepared the coup d'état in Russia, and who between September 21 and October 4 carried it out, was already widely known. Our task was not to counterpose an alternate version, corresponding to the views of the people who met with defeat. As far as possible, we aimed to set forward the facts in a dispassionate manner. We thus refrained deliberately from including in the book materials from the newspapers of the radical and nationalist opposition.

The previously unpublished eyewitness testimonies presented here are not always accompanied by the names of those who furnished them. People were wary of allowing their identity to be recorded in a published work. However, these names are known to the people who secured the testimonies. We cannot guarantee that the statements of the eyewinesses are 100 percent accurate, but we guarantee that the text published here is what these people actually said. To the eyewitnesses who agreed to testify, and to the people who recorded their statements, we express our sincere gratitude.

Alexander Buzgalin
Andrei Kolganov

1
PRELUDE

Many people would like to forget the volleys of tank fire that resounded through the sunny Moscow morning of October 4, 1993. Or else, they would like to dismiss the events of October 3 and 4 as no more than a frightening dream, a bizarre accident intruding into the political history of today's Russian rulers. But for people who are anxious to ensure that this "accident" does not become a commonplace of Russia's political life, it is important to ask: was this "accident" not the result of factors that were anything but fortuitous, and which remain capable, at the next turn in the political struggle, of confronting us with still more terrible events?

We cannot, therefore, limit ourselves to relating what occurred in Russia during those memorable September and October days. Our account must begin much earlier.

RUSSIA'S POLITICAL CRISIS

The collapse of the Communist Party, the disintegration of the USSR, and the beginning of radical market reforms provided the historical conditions leading to the deep economic, social, and political crisis with which Russia is now stricken.

By the beginning of the 1980s, not just the small section of the intelligentsia that had long criticized the regime, or a few of the most far-sighted of the regime's functionaries, but ever broader strata of the people themselves had begun to recognize that the Soviet system was a historical dead end. Both to socialism's supporters and its opponents, the existing society provided graphic evidence of the failure of the USSR's socialist experiment. For some, this proved the need for a struggle to transform the system into genuine socialism, while others interpreted it as a powerful argument against any kind of socialism or communism.

Real Socialism

In the strict sense, the society that existed in the USSR should never have been called socialist. The revolutionaries of 1917 set out to build socialism in a country which was still only semi-capitalist, and which was far from possessing the most developed industries of its time. Moreover, Russia was isolated from the rest of the world, which continued to develop within the framework of the capitalist economic model. As might have been expected, the attempt was basically unsuccessful. The revolution could not ensure that power remained with the majority of the people, and failed to prevent control over society from becoming concentrated in the hands of the bureaucracy. More precisely, the working class and the other strata of toilers in the Russian society of the time were unable to capture real power, which the bureaucracy proceeded to usurp.

In these political circumstances, a flawed strategy for economic change took shape. Bourgeois and pre-bourgeois economic relations were partly destroyed, but were by no means annihilated. The economic system that was proclaimed to be socialist in fact consisted of a colossal bureaucratic superstructure imposed on a complex web of precapitalist, capitalist, state capitalist and socialist economic relationships. Yes, elements of socialism were present. The powerful revolutionary movement of the working class did not pass from the scene without leaving a trace. However, the dominant positions won by the bureaucracy allowed it to block attempts at free socialist association by working people. Genuine efforts at workers' self-organization were subjected to bureaucratic control. Meanwhile, sharp restrictions were placed on the tendency, which had appeared on a broad scale during the initial stage of "constructing socialism," for mass creative activity in the social and economic fields.

The fresh shoots of socialism were crushed by bureaucratic control; they were restricted and deformed by pressures from the party-state apparatus, and failed to acquire decisive significance. The economic preconditions of socialism that had become established within the framework of the bourgeois system (various types of cooperation, free trade unions, joint stock enterprises, and so on) were also undermined or destroyed by the bureaucracy. This meant that the elements of the socialist system that arose were extremely weak. From the very first they were infected with the virus of totalitarian-bureaucratic degeneration.

Almost every economic component of real socialism presented a motley array of ill-assorted elements, permeated by the direct intervention of the bureaucracy in economic matters. State enterprises displayed elements of state capitalism (workers were hired employees of the state administration); of socialism (a broad system of social welfare benefits); of private capitalism (dealings by the management on the black market); and even semi-feudal elements (the system of residence permits, which together with the system under which a whole range of material benefits were provided through the enterprise, limited the free mobility of labor).

In the same way, the collective farms combined state capitalism with elements of cooperative democracy and with small-scale private production by the collective farm workers (on the individual plots where about a third of all agricultural production took place). This individual production was in effect parasitic on the social production carried on by the collective farm. However, the collective farm worker could not pursue this private production unless he or she was a member of the collective farm and took part in socialized production. This is reminiscent of semi-feudal relations.

It is thus clear that the Soviet Union did not have a mixed economy consisting of several more or less clearly defined economic sectors. What existed was a kind of salad, a chaotic mix of bits and pieces of diverse systems. The economy had reached different levels in different sectors, and even different levels within sectors. The force that served to bind this chaos together was state ownership of the economy, which in formal terms was almost complete. State ownership ensured totalitarian control by the bureaucracy over all the elements of the economic system.

The society of real socialism had no clearly delineated social structure. The general counterposition of workers to the bureaucracy was, of course, insufficient to provide a characterization of the basic social groups within this society. The complicating factor was that in this society large social classes, differing from one another in their fundamental social and economic attributes, had not come into being. Just as the economic system consisted of a multitude of heterogeneous elements, so every individual could be categorized on the basis of numerous and diverse social characteristics. A hired worker might simultaneously be a dealer on the black market, or an independent petty producer, or a member of the party bureaucracy. Because of people's ill-defined social status, various local and corporative social ties, especially links with representatives of the bureaucratic hierarchy, came to play an increased role.

It was easier to categorize people not on the basis of their formal status, but of their social and psychological orientation. This might consist of conformist submission to the bureaucracy, or of maintaining the tradition of revolutionary enthusiasm and claiming a deciding voice in social life. In the case of the ruling elite, the orientation might be toward total bureaucratic hegemony or toward a paternalistic relationship with workers. One of the most lamentable results of decades of bureaucratic rule was the broad incidence of a conformist type of social psychology.

Stagnation

The economic and political system in the Soviet Union was sometimes termed "the mobilization economy." This system was, in fact, quite effective for solving problems which demanded the rapid concentration of the nation's human and material resources for carrying out massive tasks on a large scale. Such tasks included the restructuring of the economy during the years of industrialization; economic mobilization during the Second World War and the swift conversion of industry to civilian production after the war ended; and the creation of the atomic and aerospace industries during the 1950s. Another advantage of this system was the effective centralization of the funds of the state-owned economy in the budget; this made it possible to ensure a high level of financing for education, health care, science, and culture, and in this way to create additional favorable conditions for economic growth.

As time passed, however, these advantages began gradually to be lost. This had already become noticeable by the beginning of the 1960s. The command economy gradually eroded, as various bureaucratic groups, pursuing their own narrow corporate interests, freed themselves increasingly from centralized control. Meanwhile, the central bureaucracy effectively transformed itself into little more than a series of representatives of local and sectoral bureaucracies. The efficiency of the centralized administration declined, and its decisions came increasingly to represent compromises between various groups within the bureaucratic elite. The system's capacity for mobilization, together with its ability to concentrate and quickly redistribute resources, declined sharply.

The growth of the bureaucracy, its more and more open pursuit of privileges, and its increasing contempt for the terms of the trade-off—social welfare in exchange for power—that made bureaucratic rule possible, all served to create a growing disappointment within the toiling classes. At the same time as the efficiency of the economy was gradually declining, the specific weight of budget spending on social and cultural needs was falling as well. The antagonism between the bureaucracy and the workers deepened. Bureaucratic methods of rule ceased to be regarded as a necessary evil, and every case of bureaucratic arbitrariness gave rise to greater anger.

For many years the real ideology of the bureaucrats had in practice differed sharply from the communist phraseology in which it was cloaked. Even such motivations as power, career prospects, and prestige were crowded out by the motive of personal material success. Because the established framework of the bureaucratic hierarchy and official slogans stood in the way of attaining this success, the bureaucracy came increasingly to be drawn into illegal business. Making use of their official positions, state functionaries provided protection for dealers on the black market. In this manner, an alliance came into being between the corrupt bureaucracy and criminal capital.

The Collapse of Real Socialism

Dissatisfaction grew at all levels of society. The workers and peasants were angered by the contempt which the bureaucrats showed for the interests of other social strata, by the bureaucracy's inept economic management, and by its glaring privileges. The intelligentsia were dissatisfied with the suppression of freedom of thought, and with the impossibility of criticizing the untalented official leadership. The bureaucracy chafed against the conventions imposed on it by the Soviet socialist state. A section of the bureaucracy saw in this general dissatisfaction a threat to its rule, and was ready to resort to reforms in order, after sacrificing ideological conventions and the older generation of the elite, to continue wielding power. The Gorbachev era began.

Gorbachev's policies, marked by relatively decisive steps in the area of political democracy, proved far less successful in the field of economic reform. In 1989, the collapse of the Eastern European economic union and the shift (under pressure from the International Monetary Fund) to trading with the countries of Eastern Europe on the basis of accounts in freely convertible currency dealt the first perceptible blow to the Soviet economy. Subsequent blows were dealt by unsuccessful economic experiments which, while failing to create conditions in which market regulators could operate, destroyed the previous system of bureaucratic regulation. Together with efforts by the republics of the USSR to assert their independence, and Gorbachev's unclear and inconsistent policies on this issue, these economic experiments led to numerous breaches of agreements reached earlier, refusals to make payments into the union budget, and so forth. Stagnation threatened to turn into crisis.

Gorbachev's reforms were at first conducted using slogans calling for the renewal of socialism, and even included some concessions to workers, such as expanding their participation in decisionmaking at the enterprise level, and creating Councils of Labor Collectives. In 1990, however, a clear turn took place. The words "market economy" and "privatization" appeared in

Gorbachev's vocabulary, and in the summer of 1990 the rights that had been granted to workers in 1988 were taken back. Such maneuvers did not add to the popularity of the Communist Party either among adherents of socialism, or among supporters of "the market" (few Russians at that time spoke openly of capitalism). The marketeers saw in the anticommunist opposition people who were ready for a far more radical shift to capitalism. Yeltsin, who at first also campaigned beneath the banner of socialist renewal, entered into an increasingly close alliance with the anticommunist opposition. Seeing how the positions of the Communist Party were growing weaker, a significant part of the bureaucracy aligned itself with the opposition as well.

The timid efforts to adapt the CPSU to political struggle within a multiparty system were sabotaged both by the supporters of capitalism, who had no need of an effective communist or socialist party, and by the conservative party bureaucracy, which wanted no changes at all. The word "socialism" was discredited not only by decades of totalitarian rule, but also by the absurdities of perestroika. Society became split into conservative communists and progressive anticommunists, while supporters of one or another variant of democratic socialism remained a clear minority.

The conformism of the bulk of the population, a holdover from the decades of totalitarian rule, seemed at first glance to have been replaced by mass political activity. Within this mass activity, however, an element of conformism remained. Even in the years from 1987 to 1989, when participants in unsanctioned meetings around demands for democratic rights risked no more than two weeks in jail and a few blows with a club, these meetings attracted only small groups of political activists. The meetings began drawing tens of thousands of participants only when they came to be permitted, at first de facto and then officially, and when an overwhelming section of the mass media began impressing on people day in and day out that taking part in democratic meetings of an anticommunist and anti-government slant was the duty of every honest citizen.

Yeltsin's victory in the 1991 presidential elections showed clearly where the sympathies of the population lay. Bureaucrats switched to the Yeltsin camp in large numbers, and Gorbachev's authority fell sharply. The bizarre putsch of August 1991 merely accelerated the process. The bulk of the bureaucracy swiftly became anticommunist. Workers could not see any point in defending Gorbachev against Yeltsin, since in their pronouncements on the economy the two leaders were now promising the same thing—the market and privatization. Yeltsin was also promising to put an end to the power and privilege of the Communist Party hierarchy. The party turned out to be incapable of putting up resistance, and Gorbachev also surrendered power without a struggle. No one was any longer preventing the regional bureaucratic elites from dividing up the USSR among themselves.

Possible Futures

Until our society sinks totally into ruin, the possibility remains of choosing between various models of its future development. Meanwhile, the earlier pattern of development and its lamentable results, together with our position in the world community, imposes a variety of limitations. Within the field of permissible options, the choice is dictated above all by socioeconomic forces, and to a lesser degree, by political ones. Some of these forces, by virtue of their character, take considerations of economic efficiency and/or social justice into account; others, meanwhile, ignore such matters.

The field of permissible options for our future is limited by a central contradiction. At one pole of this contradiction is Russia's status as a southern country in the economic sense. Ours is a developing country dominated by traditional industrial and preindustrial technologies for extracting and processing raw materials, assembly operations, and so forth. Russia possesses a bureaucratic, dependent capitalist class, oriented toward comprador activity. The population is socially passive, differentiated according to its degree of closeness to the corrupted layers of the bureaucracy, and subordinated to the new nomenklatura. Our country's sociocultural potential is slowly declining.

At the other pole of the contradiction we find the maintenance and development of postindustrial (high) technologies on the basis of mutually advantageous cooperation with the world community, in the framework of a primarily industrial economy. Here we also find the transformation of the present socioeconomic salad into a mixed system of productive relations with a high level of socialization (inheriting the real elements of socialism), and on this basis, the debureaucratization of the economy and its institutions. We find some features of a democratic social and political system—that is, one which could ensure genuine popular rule. We find priority given to humanitarian, ecological, and cultural values.

The most likely scenarios include a number of others that do not arise from the counterposition of these extreme variants.

First are two models of nomenklatura capitalism. Those who dislike Marxist terminology might prefer the description "nomenklatura civilism." This system differs from a civilized market economy in one vital respect: economic and political power belongs to the nomenklatura. Of the two models here, model A is a Western variant, and model B a patriotic one. In model IA, Western nomenklatura capitalism, the new generation of the nomenklatura, together with a specifically Soviet middle class, would exploit the passivity of the broad white-collar sector, and after gaining top positions in economic institutions, bring about a slow evolution of the elements of the former state capitalism and the underground market toward a market economy dependent economically and technologically on more developed countries. A nomenklatura-corporate system of property and economic regulation would dominate.

Various forms of noneconomic compulsion would slowly die out, and elements of socialism, along with the mechanisms of workers' self-organization, would deliberately be destroyed. If resistance appeared from below, a Pinochet-type model would be set in place. After fifteen or twenty years of crisis and torment for the majority of the population, we would arrive, perhaps, at the stage of middle-level development.

Model IB is patriotic nomenklatura capitalism. In its basic features it is similar to the model just described, except that the leading role within it would be played by the national technocratic elite and by the middle-level economic bureaucracy of the previous generation. This is a somewhat different social force, and hence the result of its rise to power would be a far more autarchic and economically archaic system of production, involving bureaucratic regulation and technocratic-managerial, semistate forms of property and power. For all its shortcomings—above all, the fact that it represents a historic dead end—this model could help in the short term to prevent a catastrophic crisis and to maintain, at least in part, the country's technological and humanitarian potential.

The second scenario involves a reactionary struggle to restore the old inorganic, crisis-wracked system, arising on the basis of semifeudal relations and bureaucratically deformed elements of socialism. In historical terms this option has no prospects whatsoever, but in the short term the social forces supporting it—above all, state employees accustomed to the secure life of the past, along with such sociocultural tendencies as the growth of patriotic moods in a context of heightened international tensions—could be important in the struggle between the two variants of the first scenario.

The third scenario is now almost inconceivable, though during perestroika it enjoyed a certain chance of success: namely, the rise of a socialist tendency based on traditions of mass social and economic creativity, and the sprouting of the shoots of socialism in our society within the context of a genuinely democratic, socialized economy. This scenario is important not only as an abstract possibility, but also because it corresponds to a real trend toward self-organization and the formation of associations of economic subjects. This trend is manifested in the trade union, consumer, and environmental movements, in efforts to develop associated, collective forms of property, and in many other phenomena.

This tendency can and must become the counterforce preventing our country from sliding into the extremely harsh and antidemocratic variants of Western or patriotic nomenklatura capitalism that threaten to emerge. These variants are asocial and ineffective where the human dimensions of the economy are concerned. Only an active and uncompromising struggle for self-organization can ensure the realization of the fourth and most desirable scenario: an extended (though not indefinite) compromise between the various social forces in our crisis-ridden economy.

Which of these objectively possible scenarios for the future development of Russia comes to be realized depends on the disposition of political forces within the country.

THE POLITICAL LANDSCAPE ON THE EVE OF THE COUP

The political system in Russia inevitably reflected all the subtle permutations of the socioeconomic salad. But this system was, and remains, a distorting mirror, since all of our political life has been and remains a product of our totalitarian past, which continues to misshape the present.

This distortion is exemplified by the extremely weak development of the population's social and political muscles. Schooled in passivity and dependence during long decades of rule by the paternalistic bureaucracy, the majority of Russian citizens not only failed to acquire the ability—characteristic of bourgeois society—to struggle actively for their interests through such vehicles as trade unions and political parties. By the beginning of the 1990s they had also finally lost the enthusiasm that marked the first builders of socialism in the 1930s, the naive romantics of the 1960s, and the genuine democrats of the 1980s. By the autumn of 1993 the political passivity of the mass of the population had reached monstrous levels. This was partly due to the deep economic crisis, which was forcing people to concentrate on the struggle for survival.

This passivity has resulted in an extremely weak level of development of the institutions of civil society—which were also undermined by the economic crisis—and of the forms of popular self-organization. In the great majority of cases the political parties did not have more than a few thousand members, and the largest had only a few tens of thousands. Within the parties, the groups of political leaders numbered at best one or two hundred people, who moreover had extremely weak links to the membership base. The social movements suffered from the same illness: the majority of trade union, women's, environmental, and similar organizations functioned in effect as apparatus structures, lacking serious support from below and, as a result, incapable of any serious political activity.

Also, a highly peculiar set of political forces had come into being in Russia by October 1993. One of the direct causes of Yeltsin's victory and the opposition's defeat is to be found here.

The totalitarian past of our transitional society, which now unites the remnants of mutant socialism, state capitalism, and non-economic compulsion with a nascent corporate-mafia (nomenklatura) capitalism, has been crucial for determining the specific features of the political landscape in Russia. In our country the division of political forces into leftists (from communists and socialists to social democrats) and rightists (from liberals to monarchists and fascists) that is traditional for capitalist society is gradually taking shape. But another highly significant basis for division has also appeared. On one side are supporters of the maintenance or restoration of the totalitarian-bureaucratic mechanisms of power which feed off either the mutant-socialist or the nomenklatura capitalist socioeconomic system, and on the other are those who fight to break down the old model so that democracy and popular power can triumph.

This second basis for division cuts in two both leftists and rightists in Russia, creating such paradoxes as a bloc of fundamentalist communist organizations and nationalists of all stripes, from Constitutional Democrats and Christian Democrats to monarchists.

In practice, the political map is divided into four quadrants (see Figure 1–1). Each of these sectors includes a multitude of different organizations constantly drifting in one direction or another.

The main social and economic base for the communist fundamentalists has been the fragments of mutant socialism, which give rise to nostalgia for the totalitarian-socialist past. This is not only an ideological tendency, but also a material one, taking the form of a particular model of social and economic behavior. It perpetuates a conservative, conformist position that is especially widespread among the socially undefended sectors of the population.

These fragments of mutant socialism that have survived to the present day are capable of arousing a progressive desire to preserve the real achievements of the past: above all, social guarantees and elementary collectivism. But as a rule, this desire is manifested in the false shape of parasitic appeals to the authorities to provide a guaranteed minimum of vital requirements; this is the source of much of the popular support for progovernment political tendencies.

By contrast, the communists and socialists of the democratic camp arose as political forces expressing an objective worldwide tendency toward the socialization and democratization of the economy and politics. They try to base themselves on the weak but authentic elements of workers' self-organization and creative social activism—trade unions, collectively owned enterprises, and organs of self-management. The weakness of these elements, together with the conformism of the majority of the population, was responsible for the narrowness of the social base of the democratic left forces in Russia on the eve of the October coup and in its aftermath. These factors are also responsible for the weak and contradictory nature of the actions of the democratic left during this period.

During 1993 the camp of the bourgeois democrats in Russia was split into at least two parts. On the right were pro-Yeltsin political parties and organizations, above all Democratic Russia and the electoral coalition

Figure 1-1: Quadrants of the Russian Political Map

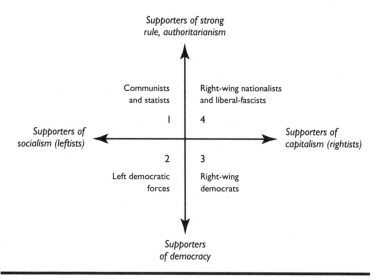

Russia's Choice that was formed on its basis, which advocated "shock therapy"—rapid transition to a market economy through limitation of state intervention, strong deflationary policies, tight controls on the volume of money circulating, and sharp decreases in government expenditures (especially social spending). This camp was evolving in the direction of support for either McCarthyism or a Pinochet-style dictatorship. On the left (in this case, closer to the center) were a group of reformist parties and organizations, most notably the Civic Union.

The centrists from the Civic Union and the forces close to it rested mainly on the paternalistic-minded bureaucracy and on the semi-statized entrepreneurial sector—that is, directors of large industrial enterprises, which were suffering deep declines and a total crisis of indebtedess as a result of shock therapy. Unlike the raw materials sector and commercial-financial capital, which supported Yeltsin, the industrialists lost out both from the government's pro-Western orientation and from the forced transition to the so-called particular market, which was deepening the already huge disproportions in the economy. This was the case for directors of both state-owned industrial enterprises and formally privatized firms—that is, those that had become joint stock companies.

However, the oppositional sentiments of this sector were heavily undermined by the opportunities which large industrial enterprises enjoyed for profitably exploiting their monopoly positions. Under conditions of price liberalization, some of the entrepreneurs possessed ideal conditions for amassing capital at an accelerated rate.

The centrists also received significant support from some skilled workers and members of the intelligentsia who hoped to prosper through selling their labor power advantageously under the conditions of a social market economy, rather than aiming to profit from speculation.

Socially and economically, Yeltsin's support base was and remains diverse. The president's backers include the new generation of the nomenklatura, mainly children and grandchildren of middle- and higher-level functionaries. This generation grew up amid the decay of Brezhnev's socialism. It was Western-oriented, cynical, devoid of paternalist illusions, and extremely dissatisfied with the fact that during the perestroika years it was denied a share of the pie, or received disproportionately little.

A second group of Yeltsin supporters arose on the basis of shadow capital. This group transformed itself into the "banditocracy"—a sector made up of participants in newly legal organized criminal activity, intermingled with corrupt officials. Now, it is gradually transforming itself into a corporatist-mafia bourgeoisie. This group is supplemented from below by new entrepreneurs—the engineers, economists, and others who have successfully taken up such speculative activities as financial and commercial brokerage operations, trade in real estate, and so forth.

A third, relatively small group of Yeltsin supporters is made up of members of the elite intelligentsia who have benefited substantially from switching—yet again—to the side of the victors.

Finally, the most important support for Yeltsin comes from a mass of small-minded, consumption-oriented people who in place of the old myth about communism, under which benefits were supposed to flow in a broad stream, have accepted the myth of the market, according to which every decent citizen, if he or she does not become a millionaire tomorrow, will at least live like the decent citizen of the USA. These people are staff members in elite establishments, members of the worker aristocracy (mainly in the area of raw materials and fuel extraction), and workers in joint

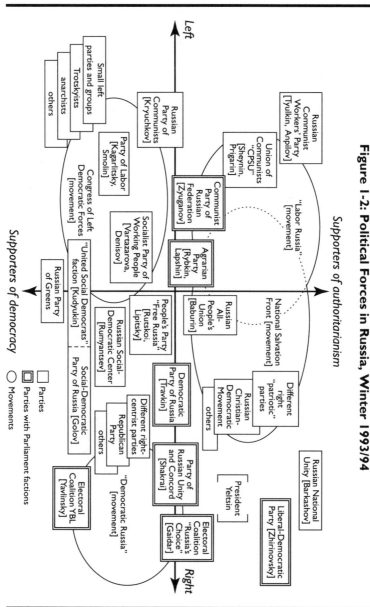

Figure I-2: Political Forces in Russia, Winter 1993/94

ventures, banks, and other commercial structures that enjoy a relatively privileged position under the conditions of nomenklatura capitalism.

Support for right-wing political organizations of a nationalist and semi-fascist stripe has come from conformist elements at all levels of the population, which in the course of the economic crisis has been subjected to a rapid lumpenization. Many Russian citizens have been accustomed for decades to depend totally on one or another leadership, and to surrender all their political and economic rights to it. Under conditions of extreme crisis, angered by a sense of national humiliation following the disintegration of the USSR, and after losing familiar values and ideological reference-points, such people have often proven capable of supporting semi-fascist slogans such as the call for the "heavy hand," which supposedly would solve all the population's problems on its behalf. To many Russians disappointed with the policies of the democrats, it seemed worthwhile in 1993 to strike a deal with the authorities along the following lines: "You guarantee me order and a bearable life, and I'll give you all my rights and promise to work in a disciplined way."

Figure 1–2 shows roughly where the structures corresponding to these various currents were located on the political map of Russia in the winter of 1993–1994.

Nostalgia for a Strong State

As the main link in the former USSR, Russia is a historically established superpower, possessing a vast potential in technology, raw materials, the humanities, and the military. At the same time, and perhaps as a result, it is oriented toward a relatively autarchic pattern of economic development. In striking contradiction to its potential, however, Russia is evolving toward the status not simply of a backward but of a rapidly de-developing economic subsystem of the world economy, within which it plays the role of a raw materials appendix offering extremely cheap raw materials and labor power.

Another factor has now been superimposed on Russia's geopolitical situation. The destruction of the former, highly ideologized society has created a vacuum of ideas. This ideological black hole has proven especially important in Russia, with its traditions of intensive spiritual life and its perennial conflict of Westernizing and Slavophile ideas. At a time when socialist ideas are in crisis, and Russians are quickly becoming disillusioned with liberalism, the ideological vacuum which has appeared is most readily filled by national-statist concepts.

The Russian people, who traditionally have been oriented mainly toward a collective rather than an individualist way of life, have in practice found only one form of community intelligible—a national one. All other social—rather than state—mechanisms have either collapsed from their own rottenness, as in the case of bureaucratic structures such as the CPSU, or have been destroyed by the emerging nomenklatura capitalism; this has been the fate of the organs of self-management, and of many popular organizations.

Finally, one must also take account of the fact that the national-ethnic formations on the territory of our country, whether Russian, Tatar, Jewish, or whatever, have fallen into a state of ideocultural decay as a result of the commercialization and Westernization of the values and culture that nurture the life of the soul.

The oppressed but conformist majority of working people in Russia were thus gripped by a nostalgic yearning for a strong state that would guarantee social security, and also by a weariness with the growing disorganization of society, above all the criminalization of all fields of life. Nationalism and statism, in the form of a law-and-order mentality, became a sort of supra-class factor which did much to determine the structure and real influence of various social forces during the summer and autumn of 1993.

As a result, the disposition of forces on the eve of the October events was roughly as follows.

The president, the executive power supporting him, the "new Russians" and the market-oriented sector of the population made up an unstable social and political structure. The precariousness of the advantage enjoyed by the presidential camp was shown by the April 1993 referendum, when, despite the pro-Yeltsin bias of the mass media, the vote in favor of the president was not especially impressive. Of those who turned out, 58 percent supported Yeltsin personally, and barely half—52 percent—voted in support of his policies.

The opposition was close to victory, but was extremely fragmented, and rested not only on democratic and socialist moods and social forces, but also on conservative statist and nationalist ones. As a result, the people's deputies of Russia, the political parties making up the opposition, and the sectors of the population that did not support Yeltsin were divided and unorganized.

Meanwhile, between the winter of 1992–1993, when the Seventh Congress of People's Deputies removed Gaidar from the post of Prime Minister and the parliamentary majority moved into confrontation with Yeltsin, and the following summer, when the parliamentary centrists headed by Khasbulatov went on the offensive against the president, the relationship of forces shifted gradually in favor of the opposition.

One of the most important factors behind this shift was the gradual working out of a coordinated left-centrist program of the democratic opposition. It rejected shock therapy, and favored a gradual transition to a regulated social-market economy. Its political slogans included calls for a parliamentary republic and for a social contract—a Russian variant of the Moncloa pact. Its social base was some of the national entrepreneurs, and the majority of workers, who were suffering terribly as shock therapy was applied and the crisis deepened (leading some of us to refer to the policy as "shock without therapy").

The consolidation of the opposition forces on this basis had begun, but it proceeded extremely slowly, and was torn by contradictions. As a result, the Yeltsin team realized that they still had a final chance. The April events had shown that the president and his supporters could no longer win by peaceful methods. The choice that remained was between renouncing the pillage of the country, and staging a military coup d'état. This assertion, of course, requires further proof.

Authoritarianism and Shock Therapy

The notion of an authoritarian regime as a prerequisite for Russia's transition to the market appeared long before October 1993. Several years before the coup, scholars aligned with the democratic socialist forces—including the authors of this book—were not only writing of this danger but also speaking out publicly on it, because the logic of the system's development had long pointed to such a threat. The Programmatic Declaration of the Party of Labor, drafted during the second half of 1992, already predicted openly that the president would disperse the parliament, abolish the system of soviets, and cease paying any heed to the law.

During the winter of 1991–1992, ideological preparations for the introduction of a right-wing authoritarian regime began. Not only advisers to Yeltsin, but also journalists who styled themselves "democrats," and members of the intelligentsia who considered themselves liberal-thinking, whitewashed and publicized the experience of the Pinochet regime. They instilled the idea that the end (the market) justified the means (denial of human rights, suppression of trade unions, and so on) in popular consciousness.

During 1992 the question of restricting the rights of the trade unions was raised repeatedly in Yeltsin's circle. Opposition meetings and demonstrations were repeatedly banned. On February 23 and June 22, 1992, and on May 1, 1993, this led to clashes between the militia and demonstrators. In March 1993, Yeltsin made his first attempt to restrict the powers of the parliament.

What was the cause? What was the reason that compelled Yeltsin, who not long before had been a high-placed party official, to recall the old methods of crushing democracy? Why were his supporters among the new nomenklatura and the nouveaux-riches "new Russians" solidarizing with a Communist chief from the Brezhnev era?

In fact, the old traditions of totalitarianism—above all the fantastic passivity of the population—accorded with the task of deepening the shock reforms. They served the new aims of the old masters and their newly-emerged followers.

These aims were quite different from those that the ideology of reform, and the godfather of the policy of shock therapy Yegor Gaidar, were proclaiming to the public at large. We have cause to doubt that all the people who acted in the spirit of the recommendations of the International Monetary Fund received what they had been promised. They had earlier declared cynically in private conversations that the main task of the reforms was to bring society to the "point of no return." The term, from aviation, refers to the point at which an aircraft can no longer return to its starting point for lack of fuel. Will the aircraft of the market economy succeed in landing on a new airfield, and does such an airfield even exist? What will happen to the passengers in the event of a forced landing, and do the pilots even intend to bring the aircraft down intact? All this is unknown, and is unimportant to the people who planned the flight and who are now sitting in the cockpit. They—the nomenklatura elite that, to a large extent, remain in power—have parachutes.

These people brought the economy to the point of no return in full consciousness that there would be economic, social, cultural, and inter-ethnic crises, and that most of the population would be impoverished. They did this cynically. For the benefit of the simple-minded, they drew up programs such as the 500 Days of Grigory Yavlinsky—the first economic program of radical transformation of the planned economy into the market economy. Yavlinsky has recently been taken out of mothballs even though he was no less responsible for propagandizing the market reforms than Gaidar, who put Yavlinsky's recipes into effect in such grotesque fashion. During election campaigns, they made promises that they could not keep and had no intention of keeping, just like present-day President Yeltsin and his associates in the parliament and the regions. They shifted the blame for their failures onto the next pawn or even bishop, which they could then if necessary surrender to their opponents.

Why was it obvious that the reforms would merely intensify the crisis, and if this were the case, why were the reforms propagandized and implemented by people such as Yavlinsky, Yeltsin, and Gaidar?

The fact that shock therapy had to fail, and that it was impossible to cure the genuinely sick economy of real socialism through such methods, was demonstrated long ago by numerous economists both in Russia and elsewhere. The arguments are as follows:

The supermonopolized economy of a former socialist country responds to the liberalization of prices with hyperinflation and cuts in production. Meanwhile, transforming state monopolies into private ones frees them from any control whatsoever.

Allowing the process of primitive accumulation of capital to go ahead in a context marked by huge disproportions (for example, in the structure of prices on the domestic and world markets) inevitably redirects the great bulk of capital into the sphere of exchange (that is, speculation), and especially into foreign trade, where the average rate of profit is several times higher than in production.

The destruction once and for all of patterns of life established over decades, together with abrupt falls in living standards, cannot fail to bring about a rise in social tensions, political struggle, and legal arbitrariness. In such circumstances, it would be naive to expect buyers and sellers to display rational behavior in the marketplace. For readily understandable reasons, the bulk of the population react to the reforms not with increased enthusiasm for their work and for business activity, but with passivity and growing desires for broad-scale social guarantees without the necessity of participation.

Economic reforms are thus pursued while maintaining the political power of the nomenklatura (within which the Brezhnev generation of officials gives way to that of Gorbachev, and then to that of Gaidar). The whole spectacle of the transition to the market is staged mainly in order to replace the old administrative power with property and capital. This cannot fail to result in the economy drifting in the direction of nomenklatura capitalism. An inefficient mixture has to arise, and does arise, of the worst features of actually nonexistent socialism (including bureaucratic privilege and arbitrariness, grave economic disproportions, indifference to social problems, and so on) with actually existing capitalism (profound social inequalities, drastic impoverishment of the masses, unprecedented corruption, the use of violence in order to accumulate capital, and so forth).

Finally, as the experience of Eastern Europe demonstrates, the extent of the decline is directly proportional to the intensity of the shock. The more radical the reforms, the more profound the crisis.

Why did Gaidar and Yeltsin head down this road, dragging the entire people behind them? Were these leaders incompetent, or naive? Did they go astray while following an unbeaten track?

By no means. They calculated very precisely the results they wanted, and they have obtained these results, though not yet in full measure. Because the new nomenklatura, the bribe-takers and the nouveaux-riches mafiosi had not yet fully realized their goals, they decided to resurrect Gaidar as a sign that they were still strong, and that the strategy of shock therapy would once again be pursued deliberately and remorselessly, rather than half-heartedly in the manner of Chernomyrdin. What were the goals of the new vice-premier?

In the first place, the forces around Yeltsin and Gaidar needed to seize power from the old nomenklatura, and exploiting the vigor of the popular antibureaucratic struggle, to concentrate this power in their own hands—that is, the hands of the new bureaucrats and nouveaux riches. Under no account was power to be allowed to pass into the hands of the people; democracy, in its etymological sense of popular power, would not be allowed to triumph. So far, the objective of supplanting the old nomenklatura has not been fully attained, and in conditions of crisis and falling living standards, the task of deepening the "reforms" has presented today's authorities with a brutal choice: either to impose a dictatorship in order to crush the population's well-merited discontent, or to abandon the remorseless application of shock therapy. The choice preferred by the people standing behind Gaidar and Yeltsin—the "new rich" business people who emerged in large part from the old nomenklatura—is no longer any mystery. These people gave up the chance to retreat, and to pass into history as cynics instead of criminals.

Secondly, and as has already been noted, it was essential not simply to seize power from the old guard, but also to exchange it in part or in full for property. To achieve this, it was necessary to bring about a devaluation of state property, combined perhaps with the opportunity to buy this property up at a discount or even obtain it for nothing. Both these aims could most easily be realized in conditions of hyperinflation (which would reduce the cost of state property, assessed at discount prices, to merely symbolic levels); of crisis (which would ruin perfectly viable enterprises); and of juridical anarchy, which would often make it possible to carry out privatization without having to outlay even symbolic sums.

Whatever the outward failures of Gaidarnomics—and by the political standards of civilized countries it has to be rated as a catastrophic failure—the fact remains that it enjoys broad support. Gaidarnomics is supported both by the political elite which holds power, and much more importantly, by relatively broad layers of society. For these layers, it is evident, the key features of the present situation—the continuing decline in production, the fall in the living standards of the population, the unemployment which is now reaching significant dimensions, and the collapse of investment which will make it impossible to overcome the crisis before 1996—do not add up to failure or catastrophe, but to success.

More precisely, all these phenomena which are so disastrous for most of the population are of no consequence to the people who have a direct interest in the Gaidar reforms. For these people, the important results of the reforms are different ones, which are not especially well publicized. In any serious discussion of the reforms, one cannot avoid the question: Who benefits? Who stands to gain from the unprecedented growth of financial and commercial capital, at the same time as industrial capital (reckoned here as all the capital involved in the production of goods and services) is vanishing at an accelerated rate? Clearly, that very financial and commercial capital. Who stands to gain from the liberalization of foreign trade that has yielded fabulous profits to exporters of fuel and raw materials, while wiping out production that depends on imports? These very exporters. Meanwhile, conditions are far from encouraging for producers of oil, gas, nonferrous metals, and so forth. Who has an interest in the feverish growth of small-scale commercial brokerage activity and petty trade (the omnipresent street stalls and kiosks)? Precisely those people who make this their business. Who benefits from the creation of a reserve army of labor? The very people who are now creating the fear that unemployment will become the main regulator of labor relations, smashing the trade union organizations in privatized enterprises, and openly ignoring labor legislation.

As can be seen, a considerable number of people have such interests. But there are many more who have gained nothing, and who merely cling to the hope that things will soon improve. Such people are terrified to admit how many times they have been fooled in the past. With each passing month, however, the dissatisfaction has grown. By September 1993 the Yeltsin supporters were faced with the threat that the opposition would consolidate its forces and emerge victorious; for this political camp, decisive actions were now indispensable. Meanwhile, the passivity among the population and the contradictions and inconsistencies of the opposition forces gave the president and his team a good chance of success.

The decisive moment had arrived.

2
CONFLICT

August 1993 was full of tension and foreboding. The president had promised in no uncertain terms that there would be a "hot" autumn, and had begun to speak of plans for an artillery barrage against the parliamentary opposition. To make sure these words would not be taken simply as rhetoric, he visited elite military units quartered near Moscow, and made generous promises of improved conditions for these units' officers and troops. Meanwhile, the opposition, relying on the "Parliamentary Hour" television program that had first gone on air during the summer, began a vigorous propaganda campaign in support of its positions.

Vice-President Aleksandr Rutskoi accused senior government officials of more than fifty cases of corruption, mostly having to do with illicit foreign trade. The great majority of these charges were recognized by the Moscow prosecutor's office as soundly based. The president responded by setting up his own anti-corruption commission, which, however, was engaged in only one significant case—attempting to prove that Rutskoi had an illegal account in a foreign bank. After the October events, Yeltsin dissolved this commission, and an investigation conducted by the Moscow city prosecutor established that the documents on which the accusations against Rutskoi were supposedly based were crude forgeries, prepared in collaboration between members of the commision and some of the very people Rutskoi had named as being implicated in corruption.

But at this time, in August and September of 1993, it was difficult for ordinary citizens to make sense of the stream of accusations and counteraccusations. In any case, the hostility between the president's team and the opposition leaders who relied for their strength on the parliament and on Vice-President Rutskoi became increasingly bitter. Everyone agreed that fierce political battles lay ahead.

THE LINES ARE DRAWN

Decree No. 1400

It was already obvious in mid-September that Yeltsin was anxious to have done with the vexatious parliament and the constitution that restricted his actions. Nevertheless, the measures he announced in his television address on the evening of September 21 came as an almost complete surprise. In his speech he proclaimed the dissolution of the Supreme Soviet and the Congress of People's Deputies, deprived the deputies of their parliamentary immunity, suspended a number of articles of the constitution, and halted the activity of the Constitutional Court. Some twenty-four hours before the speech was delivered, the parliament had been alarmed by the arrival in the capital of an extra contingent of special forces troops. The parliamentarians had even managed to show that the explanation given by Interior Minister Viktor Yerin for the presence of these troops was a complete lie. But Yeltsin had already made his decision. The fatal step was taken.

DECREE OF THE PRESIDENT OF THE RUSSIAN FEDERATION
On Stage-by-Stage Constitutional Reform in the Russian Federation

The political situation which has arisen in the Russian Federation poses a threat to the country's state security and public order.

The direct resistance to the implementation of social and economic reforms, the open and persistent obstruction in the Supreme Soviet of the policies of the popularly elected President of the Russian Federation, and attempts to directly exercise the functions of the executive power in place of the Council of Ministers show with complete clarity that the majority in the Supreme Soviet of the Russian Federation and a section of its leadership have openly begun to trample on the will of the Russian people, expressed in the referendum of April 25, 1993. This has involved gross violations of the Law on the Referendum, according to which decisions adopted by an all-Russian referendum have supreme juridical authority, do not require any confirmation, and must be applied without fail throughout the territory of the Russian Federation.

The Congress and the Supreme Soviet are making systematic and increasingly active attempts to usurp not only executive, but even judicial functions.

Meanwhile, they have not only failed until now to create a legislative basis for the implementation of the Federative Agreement, but have often taken decisions which contradict the federative nature of the Russian state.

The process of constitutional reform in the Russian Federation has been brought practically to a halt. The Supreme Soviet is blocking the decisions of the Congress of People's Deputies on the adoption of a new Constitution.

In the day-to-day work of the Supreme Soviet, the rules of this body and the order established for the preparation and adoption of its decisions are being systematically violated. In the sessions, voting on behalf of absent deputies has become a normal practice, effectively doing away with popular representation.

Violations are thus occurring of the very bases of the constitutional system of the Russian Federation: popular authority, the separation of powers, and federalism. The principle of parliamentarism in the Russian Federation is being discredited even before it has managed to rise up and consolidate itself.

In the given circumstances, there is only one step which accords with the principle of popular authority and which is capable of putting an end to the conflict between the Congress and Supreme Soviet on one hand, and the President and the Government on the other, while also overcoming the paralysis of the state power. This step is the holding of new elections for a new parliament of the Russian Federation. These elections will not represent early elections for the Congress of People's Deputies of the Russian Federation and the Supreme Soviet of the Russian Federation, and will not contradict the will of the people as expressed in the referendum of April 25, 1993.

The need for elections is also dictated by the fact that the Russian Federation is a new state, established on the basis of the Russian Republic of the USSR, and recognized internationally as the successor to the USSR.

In view of the fact that the existing constitution of the Russian Federation does not specify a procedure for the adoption of a new Constitution, political parties and movements and deputies' groups participating in the Constitutional Assembly, together with representatives of the public, have repeatedly appealed to the President of the Russian Federation to call elections for a new federal parliament.

In an effort to remove a political obstacle preventing the people from themselves deciding their fate;

taking account of the failure of the work of the Supreme Soviet and the Congress of People's Deputies of the Russian Federation to meet parliamentary standards; and

noting that the security of Russia and its peoples represents a higher value than formal adherence to the contradictory norms established by the legislative branch of power;

IN ORDER:

to preserve the unity and integrity of the Russian Federation;

to deliver the country from economic and political crisis;

to ensure the state security and public safety of the Russian Federation; and to restore the authority of the state power;

on the basis of articles 1, 2, 5, and 121 of the Constitution of the Russian Federation, and the results of the referendum of April 25, 1993,

I RESOLVE:

1. To end the legislative and managerial-control functions of the

Congress of People's Deputies of the Russian Federation and of the Supreme Soviet of the Russian Federation. Until the new two-chamber parliament of the Russian Federation — the Federal Assembly of the Russian Federation — begins its work and assumes the corresponding powers, to rule through presidential decrees and through resolutions of the Government of the Russian Federation.

The Constitution of the Russian Federation and the legislation of the Russian Federation and of the subjects of the Russian Federation will remain in force in those sections which do not contradict the present Decree.

The rights and freedoms of citizens of the Russian Federation, as set out in the Constitution and laws, are guaranteed.

2. To present to the Constitutional Commission and the Constitutional Assembly by December 12, 1993, a single agreed draft for the Constitution of the Russian Federation, in line with the recommendations of the working group of the Constitutional Commission.

3. Temporarily, until the adoption in the Federal Assembly of the Russian Federation of the Constitution and of a Law of the Russian Federation on Elections, and until the holding of new elections on the basis of this law:

— to bring into force a Statute on the Federal Organs of Power during the Transition Period, prepared on the basis of the draft Constitution of the Russian Federation approved by the Constitutional Assembly on July 12, 1993;

— to assign to the Council of the Federation the functions of a chamber of the Federal Assembly of the Russian Federation with all the powers foreseen in the Statute on the Federal Organs of Power during the Transition Period.

— to determine that the powers assigned to the Council of the Federation should come into effect after the holding of elections for the State Duma.

4. After bringing into force a Statute on Elections for Deputies of the State Duma, drafted by people's deputies of the Russian Federation and by the Constitutional Assembly:

In accordance with the said Statute, to hold Elections for the State Duma of the Federal Assembly of the Russian Federation.

To instruct the Federal Assembly to consider the question of elections for the post of President of the Russian Federation.

5. To set elections for the State Duma of the Federal Assembly of the Russian Federation for December 11-12, 1993.

6. To form a Central Electoral Commission to hold elections for the State Duma of the Federal Assembly of the Russian Federation, and to charge it, together with electoral commissions subject to it within the bounds of their competence, with the task of organizing elections and of ensuring the electoral rights of the citizens of the Russian Federation in the holding of elections for the State Duma of the Federal Assembly of the Russian Federation.

7. To instruct all state organizations and officials to render the necessary assistance to the electoral commissions in the holding of elections for the State Duma of the Federal Assembly of the Russian Federation and to put a stop to any actions aimed at frustrating the elections for the State Duma, whatever might be their source.

To lay criminal charges in accordance with article 132 of the Criminal Code of the RSFSR against any persons who obstruct the exercise by citizens of the Russian Federation of their electoral rights.

7. To pay the expenses associated with the holding of elections for the State Duma of the Federal Assembly of the Russian Federation out of the funds of the republican budget of the Russian Federation.

8. The powers of the representative organs of authority in the subjects of the Russian Federation are to remain.

9. Sessions of the Congress of People's Deputies of the Russian Federation will not be convened.

The powers of the people's deputies of the Russian Federation are hereby ended. The rights of the former people's deputies of the Russian Federation, including those related to their employment, are guaranteed.

The powers of the people's deputies who are delegates of the Russian Federation in the plenary sessions and of representatives in the commissions of the Inter-Parliamentary Assembly of member countries of the Commonwealth of Independent States are confirmed by the President of the Russian Federation.

The People's Deputies of the Russian Federation who are members of the Constitutional Commission of the Congress of People's Deputies of the Russian Federation may continue their work with the commission in the capacity of consultants.

Members of the official staff and service personnel of the Supreme Soviet of the Russian Federation are sent on leave until December 13, 1993, with their salaries continuing to be paid.

10. To propose to the Constitutional Court of the Russian Federation that it not convene any sittings until the Federal Assembly of the Russian Federation begins its work.

11. The Council of Ministers/Government of the Russian Federation will exercise all the powers envisaged by the Constitution of the Russian Federation, taking into account changes and additions introduced by the present decree, and also by legislation.

The Council of Ministers/Government of the Russian Federation will ensure the uninterrupted and coordinated activity of the organs of state administration.

The Council of Ministers/Government of the Russian Federation will take under its jurisdiction all organizations and institutions subject to the Supreme Soviet of the Russian Federation, and will reorganize them as necessary in order to prevent the duplication of the corresponding government structures. Necessary measures will be taken to provide work for employees made redundant. A legal succession will be ensured with relation to the powers of the Supreme Soviet of the Russian Federation as the founding body in all areas where the legislation currently in force makes provision for the status of a founding body.

12. Until the Federal Assembly of the Russian Federation begins its work, the Central Bank of the Russian Federation will be governed by the decrees of the President of the Russian Federation and by resolutions of the Government of the Russian Federation, and will be accountable to the government of the Russian Federation.

13. The General Prosecutor of the Russian Federation will be appointed by the President of the Russian Federation, and will be accountable to him until the newly elected Federal Assembly of the Russian Federation begins its work.

The organs of the Prosecutor's Office of the Russian Federation are governed in their activity by the Constitution of the Russian Federation, and also by the legislation currently in force, taking into account changes and additions introduced by the present Decree.

14. The Ministry of Internal Affairs of the Russian Federation, the Ministry of Security of the Russian Federation, and the Ministry of Defence of the Russian Federation are hereby instructed to take all necessary measures to ensure state security and public order in the Russian Federation, furnishing a daily report on these matters to the President of the Russian Federation.

15. The Ministry of Foreign Affairs of the Russian Federation is hereby instructed to inform other states and the Secretary-General of the United Nations that the decision to hold elections to the State Duma of the Federal Assembly of the Russian Federation has been dictated by the desire to preserve the democratic transformations and economic reforms. This decision is in total conformity with the bases of the constitutional system of the Russian Federation, and above all with the principles of popular authority, the separation of powers and federalism, and rests on the will of the people of the Russian Federation as expressed in the referendum of April 25, 1993.

16. The decree "On Stage-by-Stage Constitutional Reform in the Russian Federation" will be submitted for examination by the Federal Assembly of the Russian Federation.

17. The present decree enters into force from the moment of its signing.

I express the hope that everyone who holds dear the fate of Russia and the prosperity and happiness of its citizens will accept the need to hold elections for the State Duma of the Federal Assembly as a peaceful and legitimate way out of the prolonged political crisis.

I ask the citizens of Russia to support their President at this critical time for the fate of the country.

President of the Russian Federation B. Yeltsin

Many of Yeltsin's arguments concerning shortcomings in the work of the Supreme Soviet rested on actual facts. Nevertheless, the main justifications offered for the dismissal of the representative power were false.

Neither the Congress of People's Deputies nor the Supreme Soviet was hindering the implementation of the reforms. All the political leaders in the parliament declared their adherence to the strategy of the reforms with complete sincerity. Not a single decision adopted by the parliament amounted to a refusal by the representative power to support the executive authority in implementing the reforms. The fact that the people's deputies did not limit themselves to expressing simple approval of the decisions of the executive power, but introduced certain amendments, cannot be construed as opposition. In most cases, the deputies were denied the possibility of rejecting legislative initiatives submitted by the executive power—because there were no such initiatives. The overwhelming majority of the legislative acts which ensured that the reforms went ahead were drafted and adopted by the deputies on their own initiative.

Yeltsin's reference to the results of the April referendum was equally strange. One of the referendum questions concerned confidence in the policies of the president and the government. These policies received the support of 52 per cent of the electors who took part in the voting. Yeltsin interpreted this result to mean that all doubts as to the correctness of subsequent actions by the president and the government were forbidden, and that anyone who expressed a different opinion, or even tried in some way to modify decisions of the executive power, was acting against the will of the people. However, the will of the people was also expressed in the votes of the 48 percent of participating citizens who rejected these policies. As representative organs, the Congress of People's Deputies and the Supreme Soviet were compelled to express the interests of this sector of the electorate as well. In any case, no referendum gave Yeltsin the authority to abolish the constitution and disperse the parliament.

Yeltsin's argument that the elections for the new parliament could not be termed early elections, and that for this reason the referendum decision rejecting early elections had not been violated, was an act of violence against any kind of logic. Early elections for the Congress of People's Deputies and the Supreme Soviet would have violated the referendum decision. Thus, the president dissolved these organs of representative power, took arbitrary and one-sided decisions on the structure and powers of the new parliament, called elections for this parliament, and argued that this did not contradict the expressed will of the people!

There is no point in delving further into the sophisms of which this decree was full. It should simply be added that Yeltsin himself repeatedly violated the provisions of his own decree. For example, he decided against turning the Council of the Federation, consisting of the executive and legislative heads of government in the subjects of the Russian Federation, into a chamber of the Federal Assembly. Moreover, when it became clear that he would not win the support of the Council of the Federation for his arbitrary acts, he refused altogether to convene it. Instead, he dissolved the representative organs in the regions of the Russian Federation—again in contradiction to his own decree—and ordered elections to be held for the Council of the Federation simultaneously with the elections for the State Duma. The rights and freedoms of citizens, guaranteed by this decree, were violated frequently and arbitrarily.

Recalling the inglorious fate of the Supreme Soviet of the USSR, which ended its days without any resistance, the Supreme Soviet of Russia took a firm position. Yeltsin's Decree No. 1400 was declared invalid, and the president himself, in accordance with the provisions of the constitution, was formally relieved of his post. This decision was confirmed by a judgment of the Constitutional Court of Russia. In accordance with the constitution, Vice-President Aleksandr Rutskoi was sworn in as acting President of the Russian Federation.

JUDGMENT OF THE CONSTITUTIONAL COURT OF THE RUSSIAN FEDERATION
Moscow, September 21, 1993.

The Constitutional Court of the Russian Federation, consisting of Chairperson V.D. Zorkin, Deputy Chairperson N.V. Vitruk, Secretary Yu. D. Rudkin, and judges E.M. Ametistov, N.T. Vedernikov, G.A. Gadzhiev, V.O. Luchin, T.G. Morshchakova, V.I. Oleynik, N.V. Seleznev, O.I. Tyunov, and B.S. Ebzeev, having examined in its session the actions and decisions of the President of the Russian Federation in connection with his decree No. 1400 of September 21, 1993, "On Stage-by-Stage Constitutional Reform in the Russian Federation," and his Address to the Citizens of Russia of September 21, 1993, on the basis of article 165.1 of the Constitution of the Russian Federation, and of point 3 of section 2, section 4 of article 1, and articles 74 and 77 of the Law on the Constitutional Court of the Russian Federation, makes the following judgment:

The Decree of President of the Russian Federation B.N. Yeltsin No. 1400 of September 21, 1993, "On Stage-by-Stage Constitutional Reform in the Russian Federation," and his Address to the Citizens of Russia of September 21, 1993, are in conflict with section 2 of article 1, with section 2 of article 2, with article 3, with section 2 of article 4, with sections 1 and 3 of article 104, with section 3 point 11 of article 121.5, with article 126.6, with section 2 of article 121.8, and with sections 165.1 and 177 of the Constitution of the Russian Federation, and provide grounds for the removal from office of President of the Russian Federation B.N. Yeltsin or for the bringing into force of other special mechanisms relating to his responsibilities in line with articles 121.10 or 121.6 of the Constitution of the Russian Federation.

Chairperson on the Constitutional Court of the Russian Federation
V.D. Zorkin
Secretary of the Constitutional Court of the Russian Federation
Yu. D. Rudkin

Others Take Sides

Yeltsin reacted swiftly to the firm position taken by his political adversaries. On his instructions, various telephone lines of the special government communications network were severed, cutting off calls to and from the building of the Supreme Soviet of Russia (the White House), the Constitutional Court, the apartments of a number of eminent political figures (including some who had no connection with the opposition), and, for some reason, the General Staff of the Armed Forces of Russia. Also out of action, paradoxically, were the telephones in the offices of the Federal Center of Government Communications itself.

A demarcation of political forces began. The pro-Yeltsin parties and movements spoke out in support of the president's decree, while the organizations of the opposition and the center condemned it. The decree was also rejected by the country's largest trade union body, the Federation of Independent Trade Unions of Russia (FNPR), and by the overwhelming majority of its affiliates, including the Moscow Federation of Trade Unions.

This does not mean that all the organizations noted above supported the Supreme Soviet and its leaders. The centrist and democratic left parties and organizations, together with the trade unions, stood on a position of defending the constitution and the rule of law, speaking out in support of the so-called zero option that was also urged by Chairperson of the Constitutional Court Valeriy Zorkin. The essence of the zero option was that Decree No. 1400 was to be revoked along with all decisions of the Congress of People's Deputies and the Supreme Soviet that had been adopted since the decree was issued. Meanwhile, the constitution was to be put back fully into force, and simultaneous early elections were to be held for the president and the Congress of People's Deputies. Initially, however, the zero option was not approved by either of the contending sides.

Outside the Supreme Soviet building, on Free Russia Square, supporters of the parliamentary leaders began gathering. Activists of political parties supporting the parliament's position spoke regularly from the balcony of the House of Soviets, and so did Rutskoi and Khasbulatov from time to time. The number of people taking part in the meetings varied constantly. During the afternoons no more than two or three thousand people were present. After working hours the numbers swelled noticeably, to six, eight, sometimes ten thousand, and by late in the evenings, the numbers shrank again to a few hundred people.

Most of the people who came to give their backing to the Supreme Soviet were supporters of radical opposition organizations such as Working Russia, the Front for National Salvation, and the Russian Communist Workers Party, along with smaller organizations of a similar bent, some of them clearly extremist. The numbers and influence of the latter were small, but they were distinguished by their ultrarevolutionary or chauvinist agitation. Also on the square were considerable numbers of people who were not part of the opposition, and who had no great love for the parliament, but who thought it essential to defend the constitution. Among them were people who had stood around the White House in August 1991. The participants in the meetings began erecting barricades, at first purely symbolic, around the House of Soviets.

Rutskoi named three ministers to take the places of those who had refused, despite the oaths they had taken, to defend the inviolability of the constitution. As Defense Minister he named Colonel-General Achalov; as Security Minister, Barannikov, whom Yeltsin had recently fired from this post; and as Interior Minister, former Deputy Interior Minister Dunaev.

The Confrontation Escalates

On September 23, all of the telephones in the FNPR building were cut off. Rumors began to circulate that the funds in the union federation's bank accounts would be confiscated. Late in the evening of September 23 the first serious incident of the crisis, involving human casualties, took place near the headquarters of the Combined Armed Forces of the CIS. According to official statements of the Internal Ministry, members of the Union of Officers, headed by Lieutenant-Colonel Terekhov, attempted to seize the Combined Armed Forces premises. In an exchange of gunfire with the militia, a militia officer was killed, and in an apartment building nearby a stray bullet killed an elderly woman. Terekhov and eight other people were arrested.

Terekhov's lawyer denied a report that he had confessed to having committed the actions of which he was accused, and that he had named his accomplices. The Moscow city prosecutor's office released eight of the people arrested for lack of evidence against them. Eyewitnesses testify that the shoot-out began not at the military headquarters, but at a nearby gas station. According to the official version, the members of the Union of Officers were armed with automatic rifles, but eyewitnesses say the gunfire was from pistols.

Most of the newspapers, along with the state-controlled radio and television, publicized only the official version, which accused the leaders of the Supreme Soviet of aiding and abetting the criminals, and contributing to the bloodshed by indiscriminately handing out weapons to parliament supporters.

The facts indicate that weapons were indeed being handed out. A detachment of volunteer defenders of the White House received about forty firearms. But on September 24, Achalov placed these weapons in storage. Journalists were shown that all weapons except those in the hands of the official House of Soviets security guards were taken to armories and packed in crates. After this, a continuous line of militia was placed around the House of Soviets; at times, the militia denied people access to the building. Electricity supplies and all telephone lines to the building were cut off.

N. N., a member of a fighting detachment.
TWELVE DAYS OF CRISIS
Day One (Tuesday, September 21)
...I found the other members of the Working Russia detachment. We were standing in a group on the sidewalk. Our task, as usual, was to

maintain order. After a while the first job presented itself—we moved a drunk along.... Free Russia Square was already ringed with barricades, but they weren't all that serious, and there were many gaps in them. Altogether, they provided about as much defense as the barrier at a frontier post.

A group of us, about six people, were sent out on reconnaissance. We went along Rochdelskaya Street and down onto the Krasnopresnenskaya Embankment. Everything was quiet, and there were no militia. On the embankment there were also groups of people, campfires, and a few barricades you could walk through without the slightest trouble....

The squad commander asked people who had their passports with them to step forward. There were about twenty of us, including me.

Lists were drawn up, and then we went into the House of Soviets. Those of us in the detachment were to guard the central entrance. Then lists were drawn up again, with all passport details, so that we could be issued with weapons. The commander was a colonel, an intelligent, gray-haired man, obviously from the reserve rather than an active officer. Here there was also a group of militia from the internal guard, all of them with AKM-SU automatic rifles, and perfectly calm. They were discussing a new decision on an 80 percent pay raise. We didn't regard them with a great deal of confidence; from conversations with them, we realized it was still uncertain which way they would shoot. A hall on the first floor was set aside for rest, and a number of people were already sleeping there. I wandered about the vestibule. One group, not ours, had already received automatic rifles, eight or ten of them....

It was clear that they were making serious preparations to defend themselves. It was terrifying. I tried to estimate their chances, and decided they didn't have a hope. Behind the balustrade were a lot of dead spaces. It was impossible to position groups so as to cover these spaces and the staircase with their fire. Everything was exposed and there were high buildings all around, so the whole area would be swept by sniper fire. The House of Soviets itself was a crystal palace, all windows and doors.

By 11 p.m., the tension had begun to abate. We listened to the news on transistor radios. Shumeiko was declaring that the House of Soviets was under "self-siege." The weapons had disappeared, and people were forgetting about us....

(Supplement to the newspaper *Solidarnost* no. 23, 1993. Compiled by Petr Volkov, Lyubov Guchkova, and Vladimir Gurbolikov.)

A.I. Kolganov
EYEWITNESS TESTIMONY

I made repeated visits to the House of Soviets between September 23 and 25. The general impression I retained was of muddle and confusion. There was no precise coordination between the people taking part in meetings in front of the building, the deputies, and the apparatus of the Supreme Soviet. The leadership organs in the building and those on the square were not operating in an arbitrary way, but there was no sense that a single leadership was in control. In the building and in the surrounding area on September 23 were a motley array of irregulars with automatic rifles, organized into squads; at a guess, I would have put the total number of armed civilians at about forty. By the following day these squads had been disarmed.

The people in front of the building mainly had red flags, but there were also imperial standards and the St. Andrew's flag (the flag of Peter the Great's navy forces, now used by the right-wing Russian People's Front). A few Barkashovites (members of the semi-fascist group Russian National Unity, led by Barkashov) were there, perhaps twenty of them in all. They were conspicuous for their uniforms and their degree of organization. The numerous hand-lettered signs included some with anti-Semitic themes, and among the newspapers and pamphlets for sale on Free Russia Square there were also some with anti-Semitic content. From time to time agitators appeared among the crowd, gathering fifteen or twenty people around them and conducting anti-Semitic propaganda. They showed great irritation if anyone even tried to ask questions, let alone object. A clear majority of the signs, however, had a social and political rather than a nationalist content. I never heard any nationalist attacks during the meetings which took place almost constantly under the second-floor balcony of the White House.

The militia units that had taken up positions around the House of Soviets acted in relatively restrained fashion. From time to time, however, they would suddenly block people from going to the House of Soviets, and then just as suddenly resume letting them through. People were often forced to make their way in through courtyards, through fences and so on; this was how I got in myself. Sometimes, at places where only a few militia members were stationed, they would stand aside and let people through when groups of twenty or thirty gathered. After September 24, the regime grew more rigid. Electricity and water supplies were halted, and telephone lines cut. People could enter and leave, but food supplies could be brought in only with difficulty. A truck with diesel fuel for the emergency generator made it through on September 24 with great difficulty, and only after several attempts. The generator operated in the evenings, at first supplying current only to the communications system, which functioned via a satellite antenna that was able to connect with the city telephone network. Once darkness fell, an emergency lighting system worked for a while, but then this was turned off as well. Later, not even this functioned. Photocopiers and computers sat idle, and the internal telephone network ceased to operate.

During the balcony meetings, speakers called regularly for restraint, warning that provocations against the forces encircling the building were unacceptable, and urging people to stop anyone who tried to throw stones at the militia and so forth. A.V. Kryuchkov noted a report that someone had taken bottles of gasoline onto the barricades, which was absolutely impermissible. Among the people taking part in the meetings, rumors occasionally circulated that military units had crossed over to the side of the Supreme Soviet, but these stories were not confirmed. On the evening of September 25, however, several soldiers from the Dzerzhinskiy Division (a special division of internal troops, redeployed from their usual positions as prison guards and guards of military stocks during states of emergency) went over to the side of the Supreme Soviet. I personally saw two of them cross over, to receive a loud welcome from the meeting participants. On the following day, the Dzerzhinzskiy Division was removed from the cordon, and its place taken by the OMON—the detachment of crack riot troops from the militia.

(Manuscript testimony)

The Balance of Forces

In Moscow, the split between the executive and representative powers was extremely clear-cut. While all the higher bureaucracy supported the coup d'état, the Moscow City Soviet and all the Moscow regional soviets rejected Decree No. 1400. Pro-Yeltsin political organizations sought to mobilize mass support among Moscow residents, and organized a meeting on the basis of a Rostropovich concert which drew thousands of people to Red Square. However, these efforts were not particularly successful. A few thousand people marched to Sovetskaya Square, but they were clearly fewer than those who gathered for a meeting at the White House. The mass media overstated the number of participants in the pro-presidential meeting by several times.

If Yeltsin managed to retain control over the structures of power, he did not win the battle for moral authority in Moscow. Most of the city's inhabitants refused to take any part in a struggle between two groups of the political elite. Neither Yeltsin, who in 1991 promised to implement reforms without prejudicing the people's well-being, nor Rutskoi and Khasbulatov, who promised the same in the autumn of 1993 but failed to advance a clear alternative program to underpin their promises, could attract much sympathy. In a country without profound democratic traditions, the abstract idea of defending the constitution and legality could not arouse any important segment of the population. In Moscow, the majority were inclined to favor Yeltsin, but did not show any desire to actively support him.

The same passivity could be observed in the provinces. Meetings in support of both sides drew at most a few hundred people. Consequently, a great deal depended on the positions taken by the regional elites. The split between the representative and executive bodies in the provinces duplicated the split in Moscow. Of eighty-nine subjects of the Russian federation, the soviets in eighty-two rejected Decree No. 1400. These included the Moscow city and provincial soviets, the St. Petersburg soviet, and the soviets of practically all the autonomous republics. The majority of heads of regional administrations supported Yeltsin, but in some provinces and autonomous republics, Yeltsin's decree was rejected by both the representative and the executive bodies. In a number of Siberian provinces, the administrations declared that they recognized Rutskoi as acting President of the Russian Federation.

This does not mean that all the soviets took a stand on the side of Rutskoi and Khasbulatov. Many of them spoke out in favor of the zero option. Many of the heads of administration who supported Yeltsin simultaneously voiced support for the zero option as a means of solving the conflict. It was obvious that the provincial elites did not want either of the political groups in

Moscow to be strengthened too much, and they hoped to use the conflict to strengthen their independence from Moscow. Although all of them declared their support for the principle of federalism, they were clearly anxious to transform the Council of the Federation into an organ for political bargaining with Moscow.

The Supreme Soviet, the objectively weaker side in the conflict, gained from the position adopted by the regional bodies. Yeltsin bluntly rejected the zero option, and also the idea of simultaneous early elections for the president and parliament. The Tenth Extraordinary Congress of People's Deputies resolved to call for simultaneous early elections, though it did not agree to the zero option, considering that there were dangers in allowing Yeltsin's presidential powers to continue. A variant was discussed that would have seen the simultaneous resignation both of Yeltsin and of Rutskoi; but one way or another, the Supreme Soviet's position turned out to be closer to that of the regional elites than the hard line Yeltsin was following.

Yeltsin intensified his pressure on the Supreme Soviet, trying to alter the situation to his advantage before the sitting of the Council of the Federation due to be held in Moscow early in October. Talks that were supposed to lead to the defenders of the Supreme Soviet surrendering their weapons effectively achieved nothing, despite the signing of a preliminary agreement; the people's deputies held that this agreement failed to sufficiently guarantee their security. Yeltsin organized a total blockade of the House of Soviets. A barrier of street-cleaning vehicles was placed around the building, rolls of razor wire were strung out, and a double cordon of militia, OMON, and Interior Ministry forces was organized. In the White House, not only the telephones, the electricity, the water supply, and the heating system were cut off, but also the fire alarms and automatic fire sprinklers. Telephone lines to neighboring buildings were also switched off. The weather in Moscow turned cold, snow began to fall, and the temperature inside the House of Soviets fell below ten degrees Celsius.

Neither food, medicine, nor medical personnel were allowed through to the House of Soviets. Ambulances were unable to penetrate either to the House of Soviets or to apartment buildings nearby.

Whenever supporters of the constitution attempted to approach the cordon, let alone hold meetings, the militia and OMON cut them off swiftly and harshly. On the first day of the total blockade, September 28, a militia

Volunteers, armed with Kalashnikov automatic rifles, in the White House around 3 p.m. on October 4. Eyewitnesses report that the defenders of the White House had no heavy weapons; no more than 500 militants were armed at any time, and their weapons were limited to Kalashnikov rifles, Makarov and Stechkin pistols, a few small-caliber machine guns, grenade launchers, and carbines. Witnesses also report that Achalov, whom Rutskoi had named as defense minister, kept tight control of weapons and ammunition, only issuing them to a specially selected corps of volunteers, and refusing to distribute them until the night before the attack on the White House.

[Photo by Vojtech Lavicka]

officer died in an accident that occurred while a barricade was being dismantled on the Garden Ring Road. The accident was the result of an error by another militia officer who was driving a trailer truck. The mass media immediately blamed the death on the demonstrators and spread this lie throughout the whole country, in strident tones, for several days, even though all eyewitnesses rejected this version of the events. As eyewitnesses continued to refute the press version, the Interior Ministry was finally forced to reject it, too, but the reports of this latter development amounted to no more than a few lines of small print, and appeared only in a few Moscow newspapers.

Not long before the imposition of the blockade, the Yeltsin-controlled television showed an interview with Barannikov, the former security minister whom Rutskoi reinstated in this post. In the interview, Barannikov was shown voicing support for Yeltsin. It quickly became clear that this "interview" was a fake, put together from a recording of a television appearance by Barannikov in March 1993.

During the next four days of the blockade on the House of Soviets, the militia and OMON constantly attacked demonstrators, refusing to allow even small groups to assemble. They beat demonstrators with clubs and metal shields. They used tear gas, and threw demonstrators to the ground and kicked them, even women and old people. Recordings of radio conversations between militia members, recorded by a special group of people's deputies and a few private individuals who happened to have the necessary equipment, reveal that the militia commanders ordered their subordinates to disperse any group of citizens, and to detain as many people as possible, charging them with violations of public order. The people who were directing the militia officers over the radio constantly rebuked them for indecisiveness, and for not making enough arrests.

Testimony of Doctor of Philosophical Sciences, Professor N.S. Zlobin:
I'm a specialist in problems of social development, and what is happening in the country is important to me not just personally as a citizen, but also from a professional point of view. Our mass information media are not always unbiased, to say the least. So at ten o'clock in the evening of September 28, after attending a meeting between members of the intelligentsia and Moscow City Soviet deputies at which the actions of Yeltsin and his team were unanimously condemned as unconstitutional

and criminal, I set out for the Supreme Soviet building in order to see for myself what was happening there.

I witnessed the following:

1. The Moscow militia, although it was blocking the approaches at distant points (almost as far as the Barrikadnaya metro station), acted politely and with restraint. The next cordon consisted of OMON troops dressed in bullet-proof vests and armed with clubs and shields; some of them, I saw, had gas canisters.

2. The tens of thousands of demonstrators who had gathered taunted the OMON members, calling on them not to obey criminal orders and to let people through to the White House. But in more than two hours that I spent there, I did not see the demonstrators commit any aggressive actions or show any resistance—I stress, none whatever. All they did was to build some largely decorative barricades; I saw that trucks whose drivers were too lazy to take another route managed easily to drive through these obstacles.

3. From time to time the ranks of OMON troops shifted, dividing the demonstrators up into groups and forcing them into yards, lanes, and alleyways; then everyone returned to their previous positions. But at intervals of thirty-five or forty minutes the OMON members, after receiving some command, suddenly rushed at the stationary demonstrators, clubbing all of them in turn. It was as though they were chained dogs, and someone, crying "Sic 'em!" had let them off the leash. Previously, I had only seen such things in historical films on the actions of the Gestapo. Young people, who made up more than half of those present, generally managed to get out of the way, so the blows fell mainly on women and elderly people. I personally saw that whenever anyone who was being beaten with clubs fell down, three or four more OMON troops set upon them, continuing to beat them while they were on the ground. I saw three women beaten in this way. A man who then tried to help one of them rise to her feet was also beaten. They dragged several people off to a van, still clubbing and kicking them. Three OMON members started clubbing me as well, because I hadn't been as quick as the younger people in taking to my heels.

I witnessed three such operations; each time, the OMON troops flung themselves on the demonstrators with a sort of inhuman roar, screaming the filthiest kind of abuse, which echoed around the whole square. They dealt out the beatings in a frenzied manner and with obvious pleasure. They weren't people—they were animals, bandits. This was a provocation, launched in the expectation that there would be a response in kind that would serve as an excuse to heap blame for the much-publicized lawlessness on the demonstrators. But the attempt at provocation was a failure, perhaps because there were almost as many OMON troops as demonstrators.

4. Everything ended in a nightmarish scene. Around midnight several hundred OMON troops, again running and armed with clubs and shields, began to chase the people who remained on the street, including casual passersby, into the vestibule of the Barrikadnaya metro station. In the panic, people got stuck in the doors and then in the turnstiles. Those behind pressed on them, while the OMON members beat everyone in turn on the shoulders and heads. They hunted people down even on the escalator, making their way through to those standing lower down literally by climbing over heads and along the handrails, in the process smashing almost all the lighting fixtures. It was only because a squad of militia, headed by a colonel, blocked the OMON from continuing onto the platform, that a more terrible tragedy was averted. In such a crush, people could have fallen onto the tracks.

On the platform were people with bloody faces and hands, and with ripped clothing. On the floor, bent over, sat an old man whom one of the OMON troops had kicked in the groin. Needless to say, there was neither an ambulance on the square, nor a doctor on the metro.

I repeat: the demonstrators were unarmed. No one, absolutely no one, offered any resistance; they were chased, and they fled. This was an intentional act of cowardly, lawless vengeance, in its nature and ferocity recalling a criminal free-for-all. In a press conference, members of the Yeltsin team declared that these actions were aimed at protecting the inhabitants of Moscow from armed gangs. But the real armed gangs are the detachments of the OMON. These are law enforcement agents turned into thugs. And their bosses call themselves democrats! They have the effrontery to talk about rights and freedoms!

(Manuscript testimony)

Testimony of V.S. Savelev:

Everything began at the end of September, on the twenty-ninth and thirtieth, when the approaches to the White House were closed off. In the evenings after work I went several times to the Barrikadnaya metro station and personally saw the ranks of militia and OMON troops that were preventing people from going through to the White House. They had helmets, bulletproof vests, shields, clubs, and firearms, mainly automatic rifles.

Things got to the point where they were simply chasing people into the metro with clubs. It got to the point where they were literally committing assault and battery on people, because some of the OMON troops (it wasn't the militia, but the OMON) became extremely worked up and were bashing people without taking account anymore of who they were. It happened even to elderly people. For example, on December 1 (the Day of the Elderly, in fact) I saw several OMON members surround an old man in the metro and push him from one to another with their shields, playing a sort of game, and then pin him to the wall with their shields. When someone tried to photograph this scene, they tried to tear the photographer's camera from him, and wouldn't let him take the shot. [Nevertheless, this scene was captured on video and broadcast on television —A.K.].

We appealed to a militia major who was standing there. But he wouldn't intervene, saying simply that they weren't his people. These OMON troops were armed with automatic rifles, as well as with shields and clubs.

(Testimony tape recorded by Andrei Kolganov)

Testimony of Boris Kagarlitsky:

When the cordon around the parliament building was tightened, a total of 119 deputies were unable to enter. They established a coordinating committee which met in the building of the Krasnopresnenskiy Regional Soviet, declaring that they would continue to work there until they were reunited with their colleagues in the White House. The television promptly reported that they had gone over to Yeltsin.

To keep psychological pressure on the deputies, the Moscow city government stationed a squad of armed OMON members on the lower floor of the regional soviet building. They entered the vestibule wearing plush leather jackets over their bulletproof vests, and armed with automatic rifles and carbines—just like the characters in American movies. You could have killed an elephant with the carbines. They were met by unarmed deputies, young activists from left-wing organizations, and a few journalists. Young women asked to be allowed to hold the carbines, or to try on the bulletproof vests. The invaders were clearly nonplussed.

"So who are you?" people asked them.

"We're the Moscow OMON."

"Well go upstairs, the Riga OMON is waiting for you."

Several dozen members of the Riga OMON were in fact among the defenders of the White House, and this thought did nothing to raise the spirits of our guests. Nevertheless, the new arrivals received good-natured treatment. Not knowing what to do, they killed time reading opposition leaflets and explaining to those nearby that "everyone" needed the OMON. "When you come to power, you'll need us too." This squad soon had to be replaced.

I spent almost all that day going around the lines of the cordon, and then working with the coordinating committee. When I went out onto Krasnopresnenskaya Street late in the evening, several thousand people were marching along it in pouring rain, chanting "All power to the soviets!" There were no streetcars in sight. In front of the column marched Colonel Viktor Alksnis, giving an interview to an Argentine journalist with a bandaged head.

From the left, Interior Ministry forces appeared with shields and clubs. They tried to cut the demonstrators off from the regional soviet building. "Colonel, give your order!" shouted the demonstrators, appealing to Alksnis. Alksnis hesitated a little, and then, I thought, even seemed confused for an instant. But then he gave his order. The civilian crowd successfully executed a flanking maneuver, however, and surged around the troops from the right, preventing them from massing themselves between the regional soviet building and Krasnopresnenskaya Street.

And the resistance kept growing. Every day, several thousand people tried to break through to the White House. The troops beat them and turned them back, but others came in their place. The first barricades appeared at Krasnaya Presnya on Tuesday evening, and on Wednesday there were more of them. Activists from opposition organizations stopped trolley buses and used them to block streets. This occurred mainly on the Garden Ring Road. On the third day of these events

Muscovites were already joking that the trolley buses didn't go along the Garden Ring Road anymore—they went across it.

The Garden Ring Road was the most popular place for building barricades, but not the only one. On Wednesday evening a barricade was built next to the Belorusskiy railway station. An OMON detachment, hurriedly dispatched from the Garden Ring Road, became stuck in a traffic jam on Tverskaya Street. The OMON troops were forced to get out of their vehicles and run along the street. To do this in bulletproof vests, with weapons and full equipment, was no mean feat. When they finally reached the barricade, no one started fighting them; people simply laughed.

During the first week of the blockade, laughter was our strongest weapon. Everything was done with a good deal of merriment, and despite the dramatic character of the events, people were surprisingly good-natured. At one point Boris Kravchenko, a correspondent for the labor information center KAS-KOR, approached a group of young people who were building a barricade. He was astonished to find that the crowd was carrying the car of German labor attaché Frank Hoffer. "Don't touch that car!" Kravchenko shouted. After a short discussion, the barricade builders agreed with his arguments, and put the car back where it had been.

The demonstrators went up to the cordon, and talked to the OMON and the militia. As the rain poured down, the people in the cordon stood soaked to the skin, with mournful, helpless-looking faces. At the head of a crowd of about a thousand people, deputies of the Moscow City Soviet and of the regional soviets tried to go through to the White House. The Interior Ministry troops were ordered to beat the demonstrators. Oleg Smolin, a deputy to the Russian parliament who was blind, was unable to dodge the clubs, and received two blows—first on the back, and then on the head. Then, standing in front of the cordon, he spoke to the people who had just beaten him. The soldiers listened in confused silence. Many of them took leaflets from the demonstrators.

Moscow City Soviet deputy Andrey Babushkin was arrested by the militia—illegally, since the Moscow soviet had not been dissolved, and he retained his immunity. But when Babushkin's colleagues from the soviet, standing on the opposite side of the militia lines, heard what had happened, many of them could not suppress a smile. In 1988 and 1989

Babushkin had constantly been arrested. The militia knew him well from demonstrations on Pushkin Square; they had evidently seized him out of habit. In any case, he was well known to the militia for another reason as well; as a deputy, he had been concerned with problems of the organs of law enforcement, seeking to have apartments set aside for militia officers and helping them resolve a wide range of social problems.

"Let Babushkin go!" shouted the crowd. People answered from the cordon, "We know who he is." A few minutes later Babushkin appeared. Someone gave him a megaphone, and he delivered a fiery speech to the militia. Babushkin is not a bad orator, and they listened to him. When it was explained that militia Lieutenant-Colonel Kopeykin had seized Babushkin's deputy's card and was refusing to return it, laughter broke out both in the crowd and among the militia.

"Kopeykin, give Babushkin back his deputy's card!" shouted the demonstrators. "What do you want a deputy's card for, Colonel?" The colonel emerged from the ranks and began trying to justify himself. The militia members hid their faces behind their shields to conceal their smiles.

Over the megaphone, I related anecdotes to the soldiers, and then said: "Of course, you're not going to lay down your clubs now, you're not going to let us through to the White House, and you're not going to come over to our side. At any rate, not for the present, because the revolution hasn't started yet." Here people in the cordon again began to laugh. "But as long as we're standing here facing one another, and they haven't given you the order to beat us up again yet, let's talk for a while and try to understand why this has happened. You're defending Yeltsin's reforms. Someone's doing very well from these reforms. According to police figures, there were six Rolls Royces in Vienna in 1991. After a year of our reforms, the number of Rolls Royces in Vienna has doubled, and all of these new cars belong to expatriate Russians. Maybe you get to ride in these cars? Anyone who has a Rolls Royce, raise your club."

Then the crowd and the cordon agreed to step back a pace and form a free corridor. When both lines had retreated, someone from the crowd shouted: "There, you see how easy it is to take a step closer to one another!"

The troops were replaced. By the end of the second day of the blockade the authorities had been forced to bring reserves to Moscow from other regions; the troops were demoralized and unreliable. The commanders were above all anxious not to allow contacts between their people and the crowd. They had to keep an eye not only on the demonstrators, but also on their own forces. The tactics were changed; people were simply not allowed to gather and to enter into dialogue with the troops. At Barrikadnaya metro station, any gathering of more than five people was dispersed. Even lines at kiosks were dispersed. Everyone was driven into the metro, even non-demonstrators who lingered at the entrance. Then some people came out again, and everything was repeated. The OMON began going down into the metro and beating people right on the platform. Bewildered passengers scattered in all directions, trying to avoid the blows. It is amazing that no one was pushed onto the tracks. The injured by this time numbered in the dozens. Colonel Alksnis was taken to the hospital with a fractured collarbone and concussion. One militia officer was crushed by a colleague in a fatal accident while dismantling a barricade.

Throughout two weeks of confrontation, despite the violence of the authorities, the demonstrators did not display aggressiveness. "We don't have anything but umbrellas, so why are you scared of us?" people asked from the crowd. Not a single kiosk was overturned, and not a single shop window was broken. A few cars were overturned, but not one was set on fire. The only business to suffer any particular damage was a very expensive French boutique situated between the barricades of the White House defenders and the militia cordon. With no customers, the shop closed down for inventory. Apparently, neither the militia nor the defenders of the parliament had the money to buy the latest clothes from Paris.

(Boris Kagarlitsky. Excerpt from the manuscript of *The Square Wheels*)

A.I. Kolganov
Eyewitness Testimony (continued)

Blockade. September 28. Around the House of Soviets there were barriers made of street-cleaning trucks and coils of razor wire. A total blockade was in force. More than a hundred people's deputies of the Russian Federation were gathered in the building of the Krasnopresnenskiy Regional Soviet. Downstairs at the entrance, the Barkashovites were mounting a guard.

Somewhere between 10 and 11 p.m., after a press conference held by the deputies in the Krasnopresnenskiy Regional Soviet, I set off toward the House of Soviets with two correspondents from the KAS-KOR information center and a Swedish journalist who had just taken part in a trade union conference. We went out onto Kransopresnenskaya. We had not reached the Olymp sporting goods store before we came upon a crowd of two or three hundred people being forced back by a line of (Interior Ministry troops? OMON?—I don't know) with aluminium shields, in helmets and bulletproof vests, with clubs. The crowd argued with them, without much conviction, and departed. The clubs were hardly used.

We went on to the intersection of Zamorenovskaya and another roadway running along the side of the Krasnaya Presnya stadium. Here, about forty people were trying to talk to the troops in the cordon. Among these people were People's Deputy Andrey Golovin, and chairperson of the Cheremushkinskiy Regional Soviet Aleksandr Stepovoy, with a megaphone. The cordon was trying to force them back, and the people were retreating reluctantly; the laggards were being beaten with clubs. Several militia members surrounded the chairperson of the Cheremushkinskiy Regional Soviet, who was standing up to them, and for a minute or a minute and a half hammered him with their clubs, using all their strength. We went on to the zoo. On Krasnopresnenskaya, not far from the zoo, were remnants of three uncompleted barricades. At the intersection by the zoo was a huge pool of water with brown foam—the work of a fire brigade vehicle?

We entered the Barrikadnaya metro station. There we met I.O. Malyarov, who reported that there were barricades on the Garden Ring Road, and that traffic was blocked. Someone in the crowd said that the militia on the ring road had run over one of their own officers.

3. *Blockade. September 29.* The Barkashovites had left the building of the Krasnopresnenskiy Regional Soviet. On the ground floor the OMON were hanging around in black leather jackets, with AKM-SU automatic rifles, and some with large-caliber sawed-off shotguns. They weren't doing anything, just reminding people of their presence.

During the afternoon, small groups gathered at the cordon, trying to talk to the militia, but the militia kept forcing them away from the main cordon. Anyone who objected, or who simply lingered, was clubbed. Few of the militia showed any special zeal for this task; most carried out their orders passively, without aggression. Separate groups came out from behind the cordon and set to work with their clubs. Next to me, with a companion, was People's Deputy of the Russian Federation O.N. Smolin, who is blind. The militia forced him back along with the others, and because he failed to move fast, he received several blows with a club on the head and shoulders before we managed to shield him.

At the end of the working day there was a demonstration at the Barrikadnaya metro station. Only about two thousand people took part, and no well-known leaders were to be seen. It was between six and seven p.m., and dusk was falling. By the movie theater across the street, a group of people's deputies from various soviets were talking to the people in the cordon. Meanwhile, the cordon was slowly forcing them back. Moscow City Soviet Deputy Kagarlitsky was appealing for mutual restraint, calling on people not to use force. Around the deputies was a crowd of two or three hundred people. Kagarlitsky called on people not to press up against the cordon, but to move back a step. People complied. Deputy Marenich, from one of the regional soviets, related the circumstances in which a traffic officer had been killed on the evening of September 28. Marenich, who had personally witnessed the accident, rejected the official version according to which the man had died at the hands of demonstrators. According to Marenich, the traffic policeman fell under a trailer towed by a rig which another traffic officer was driving. The rig was moving at high speed, the trailer skidded, and the officer did not manage to leap out of the way.

The Moscow City Soviet Deputy Babushkin, who had been arrested the previous day despite his deputy's immunity, also spoke. He said that the order for his arrest had been issued by the Interior Ministry's head of administration for the northwest district (I have forgotten his name), who was standing right there, just behind the cordon. A stocky man, with an almost intelligent expression and glasses. People called on him to come discuss the question of allowing people's deputies to pass through the cordon. He refused, stating that it was impossible to get through a barrier which would take several days to clear away.

The same day, later in the evening, former People's Deputy of the USSR Alksnis was brought to the Krasnopresnenskiy Regional Soviet. He was covered with blood, and had suffered injuries to his head and to an arm. Later, the papers were to report that he had sustained a concussion and a broken collarbone. When I returned home, it was to find a doctor from the ambulance service bandaging the head of my friend Andrey Sorokin. Sorokin said he had been talking to the troops in the cordon, and when the troops began forcing him back, along with those next to him, a militia officer leapt out from behind the cordon and dealt him several blows on the head.

Blockade. September 30. The OMON changed its tactics. Groups of people who approached the cordon were now pushed back and dispersed before the gatherings reached any significant size.

Blockade. October 1. The OMON continued using the same tactic. They moved troops with automatic rifles right up to the entrance hall of the Barrikadnaya metro station. They cordoned off the square in front of the entrance, leaving only a narrow passage for entry and exit.

(Manuscript testimony)

Report by Andrey Leybov in the electronic mail conference SU.POL (fido.net), October 13, 1993:

...I am neither a communist nor a fascist; I do not belong to any party, and I am totally indifferent to Rutskoi and Khasbulatov. I went to the White House because I fear dictatorship not from the side of the crowd of deputies, but from a specific, narrow group of people. Because I am sickened by statements to the effect that "we have never had a constitution" from a man who swore to uphold this very constitution when he took his oath as president.

There were indeed followers of Barkashov at the White House, and I even counted them as they paraded. There were some seventy of them, so that handing out "thousands of firearms" to them would have been difficult.

In general, I can testify that the only people who were able to receive weapons there were people who joined the regiment formed by the Supreme Soviet, who signed the appropriate contract, and who entered real military service. The base of this regiment was made up of officers from Terekhov's Union of Officers, by Cossack formations, and by people who had come from all the various hot spots. For example, there were "White Wolves" from Serbia, a part of the Dnestr battalion, the Tiraspol OMON, the Riga OMON, and people from Abkhazia and

Karabakh. So these were not dilettantes, but people who had earlier had the right to bear arms.

...Yeltsin promised the deputies that he would virtually shower them with gold if they would just leave the congress. This was proclaimed to us day after day over a loudspeaker mounted on an armored vehicle by the Hotel Mir. The deputies were promised that they would each be allowed to privatize an apartment in Moscow, that each of them would receive a payment of twelve times their monthly salary, and that they would retain their deputy's immunity, access to special medical care, and so forth. In general, "Surrender, Russian Ivan, I'll give you a cow." [This parodies the call to surrender addressed to Russian troops by the Germans during the Second World War.] Only about a hundred and fifty deputies agreed to accept these thirty pieces of silver.

...A minor inaccuracy [this is in reply to the assertion that two thousand armed militants in the White House were surrounded by five hundred unarmed militia members]: Even at the time when the attack came, the total number of 'armed militants of the Supreme Soviet' was no greater than five hundred, and during the first days it was far fewer. Almost all of them were unarmed. Meanwhile, around them was a cordon made up of the OMON, the OMSDON [acronym for the Dzerzhinshkiy Division's official name—literally, Separate Mechanized Division for Special Purposes], and so on, half of them with automatic rifles and half with shields and clubs. The total number of people was from two to four thousand, varying from day to day. The "unarmed militia members" were also covered from all sides by twelve armored vehicles, into which ammunition was loaded before our eyes.

Nikolay Krivomazov, Nikolay Musienko, Viktor Shirokov and Vadim Gorshenin
THE FIRST SNOW IN MOSCOW SMELLS OF TEAR GAS AND BLOOD

During the night, an OMON member with a gas canister in his hands rushed after these reporters. He shouted: "Now you're going to get it, you cowards!" For some reason, the smoky pyramid of gas left the smell of raw garlic behind it. The second line of the cordon moved up to meet us as we fled. We were in a classic mousetrap: innocent and guilty alike risk their lives when they find themselves in such a situation. Fortunately, we were saved by a dark lane in the zoo. We rushed into it. The OMON couldn't keep up with us, but from behind came the roaring of a lion, as if we had awakened the king of beasts.

The animal also awakens in people when they are in a direct confrontation; this is always a pointless, terrifying situation. Those against whom mighty forces were being thrown were no longer a miserable hundred deputies. The people who were being beaten were simple mortals who had read the greetings of the American president to the Russian one, and were asking themselves with astonishment: "What would happen if Clinton decided to disperse his parliament? Who would be beating whom?"

At midnight, there was a crowd at the Barrikadnaya metro station. The people were agitated, cursing out loud. On a marble wall, someone had written in blood—blood!—the words "Yeltsin is a fascist!" "The OMON went on a spree here," an eyewitness explained, pressing a bloody handkerchief to his head. He asked that his name not be reported, since he was afraid. "The OMON drove people into the vestibule of the metro like cattle. Then they rushed after them down the escalators, smashing the lights and trampling on anyone who fell. We can only thank the militia members from the metro guard—they linked arms and stood like a wall in the way of those bandits."

"They beat everyone with their clubs, without distinction," says another man. "For example, I'm not interested in demonstrations. But when I saw a few young thugs in gray uniforms start beating up an old woman, I pulled my camera out of my bag. Then they turned on me. They ripped the camera out of my grasp, and smashed it to pieces. They threw me down onto the asphalt and started kicking me. If it hadn't been for my thick jacket, they probably would have killed me."

Then something far worse happened. It could not have failed to happen, because a mob cannot, of its nature, give rise to anything except bloodshed. Everyone tried to turn this tragedy to their own advantage. But because we were virtual eyewitnesses, we must relate everything as it actually happened.

People had unscrewed the fittings from several trolley buses in order to build barricades. Also put to use in building a barricade was a heavy electric welding apparatus on rubber tires. The militia demanded of the driver of a heavy KrAZ truck that he pull the welding apparatus out and tow it away. The driver refused. Then a militia lieutenant leapt behind the wheel and began towing the welding apparatus away himself. As the truck was moving at great speed, the load that was in tow skidded and struck the militia lieutenant-colonel and a Zhiguli car.

Someone cried out at the top of his voice: "Remember the number of the truck with the militiaman behind the wheel! Number 342! Note it down so they don't blame everything on the demonstrators!"

Witness A.B., a colonel in the reserve:

"Behind the wheel of the truck that hit the lieutenant-colonel was a militia lieutenant—I was a witness to that."

Witness A.M., sixty-eight years old:

"Yes, I lay down in front of that truck. What's a life like this worth to me, when everything's all lies. But a lieutenant-colonel came up and started trying to persuade me: 'What's all this to you, old man? Get up, for Pete's sake.' Then a few minutes later the truck came hurtling at us. The lieutenant-colonel pushed me aside, and took all the force of the blow himself...."

At three o'clock in the morning 47-year-old militia Lieutenant-Colonel Vladimir Reshtuk died. He left five children.

(Pravda, September 30, 1993)

Aleksey Tsvetkov
FREEDOM ON THE BARRICADES

Placing one hand on the Bible and the other on the Russian constitution, I swear to tell the truth and nothing but the truth.

...I saw how the OMON on the Garden Ring Road were using their clubs to bash Afghan war veterans who had forced their way through in order to defend the parliament. And I discovered there are other things you can use a shield for besides defending yourself—you can also use it to slice into the skull of an unruly element.

"*Dushmany!*" shouted a young man with a shaved head, stripped to his undershirt and covered with blood. "Bastards!" [literally, "Hellish spirits!"] One of the first to fall onto the asphalt was a punk, who had wormed his way in here somehow. Still on the ground, and entangled in the folds of his overcoat, he nevertheless managed to fling a piece of brick at the advancing OMON, for which he received a kick in the face. He lay like a wounded bird, only twitching by reflex, while they trampled on him, and where his head had been there was now only a bloody mess.

One evening on Pushkin Square, where only a few days before the kindly president had met with his adoring people, I saw bleeding women and adolescents hauled away in ambulances; they had been mercilessly beaten. I saw how people were forced to bend over on the pavement and submit to being searched; often, these people were chance passersby. If anyone raised his or her head, he or she was beaten around the ears with a shield or club....

(Obshchaya Gazeta, Oct. 29-Nov. 4, 1993)

N. N., member of a fighting detachment
TWELVE DAYS OF CRISIS
(continued)

The lights had been turned off, there was no heating or water, and it was impossible to go out for firewood. They were not letting anything through to us—no diesel fuel for the emergency generator, no food supplies, no medicine, no warm clothing that had been collected.... On the staircases, church candles were left burning so that people wouldn't break their legs. During the first two days of the blockade we received only dry rations—bread, cheese, and sometimes sausage. Once they served broth—water in which the same sausages had been boiled on a campfire....

Then there were new hardships. They drove an armored personnel carrier, painted yellow, up to the Hotel Mir. This vehicle had enormous loudspeakers mounted on it (people started calling it "the yellow Goebbels"), and they used it to bombard us with sound from 8 a.m. until 11 p.m. Our ears and heads ached; we had an almost insurmountable desire to set fire to the thing. They only read out a few texts—an appeal to refrain from violence, along with Yeltsin decrees offering benefits to deputies who agreed to desert and to workers on the staff of the Supreme Soviet. Then they cut in with some music. The repertoire was sparse—"Putana," something from the group Lyube, and other cheerful songs. Even when they announced the funeral of the militia member who had been killed at the headquarters of the United Armed Forces, they cut in immediately afterwards with the same "Putana"....

The alarm was raised. Armored personnel carriers were standing around the perimeter of the barricades. It seemed to be the latest ultimatum from Luzhkov, the mayor of Moscow. Our regiment took up its positions, but once again we were all unarmed. Markov began cursing, messengers ran around, and pressure was placed on Makashov finally to distribute the weapons they'd only been talking about.... But once again the decision on the weapons wasn't taken. The OMON were tightening up their ranks and constantly bringing in reinforcements. Markov, with an AKSU (an improved version of the Kalashnikov automatic rifle) under his jacket, went around the barricades. He called on people to stand firm and link arms. Everything else—stones, bottles, sticks—was to be used only in an extreme situation. The only thing that wasn't clear was how, in an extreme situation, we were to grab all these weapons. The time passed imperceptibly. As the assault failed to occur, the level of tension dropped....

The regiment was roused by an alarm at one o'clock in the morning. Everyone was taken to the bunker. Now they were going to arm us. Once again they checked the lists, sifting out the people who did not have passports (some had been signed up on the basis of workplace or armed forces identity cards, which did not include their registered addresses). A tense wait followed. At first we were in formation, but then we were ordered to sit. Suddenly, messengers ran in. There was a general alarm. The time was 3 a.m. We ran upstairs, lined up, and once more took up our positions. We had sticks in our hands again....

According to informed people in the House of Soviets, in addition to the regular guard, some two hundred and fifty or three hundred Cossacks and members of the Union of Officers were armed with AKSU automatic rifles, and there were also some small-caliber machine guns and grenade launchers. In addition, there were about a hundred SKS carbines, but the cartridges were mainly 5.45 millimeter. The Tiraspol group arrived with their weapons, and I saw one AK automatic rifle with a wooden stock. The other rumors about House of Soviets arsenals were probably unfounded.

(*Solidarnost* 23, 1993)

THE BOILING POINT

After October 2, events began to escape the control of both contending sides. The logic of confrontation brought passions to the boiling point. On the one side were the unarmed defenders of the Supreme Soviet, and on the other, armed to the teeth, were the militia and OMON, brought together in Moscow from throughout Russia. The forces were clearly unequal, but Yeltsin's adversaries were not about to retreat. Meanwhile, the militia and OMON, after several days of beating people with impunity, were not expecting active resistance.

On October 2, the militia and OMON attempted to disperse an officially permitted opposition meeting at Smolenskaya Square, near the Foreign Ministry building. The OMON attempted to push people out of the square even before the meeting began, and in response the people began constructing a barricade. Up to this point, demonstrators had constructed only symbolic barricades, which the militia could easily dismantle. But this was a real defense line, which the militia and OMON could not break through.

The next day, at Kaluzhskaya (Oktyabrskaya) Square, a huge group of militia attempted to prevent another officially permitted opposition meeting. Somehow—no one knows exactly why—the route from Kaluzhskaya Square to the Garden Ring Road was open, and demonstrators broke through relatively weak lines of militia and internal troops on the Krymskiy Bridge and proceeded toward the House of Soviets.

Near the House of Soviets, the demonstrators dismantled a militia barricade of trucks and razor wire without meeting any resistance. But afterwards, internal troops with machine guns opened fire from the mayor's office, which was occupied by pro-Yeltsin forces.

Smolenskaya Square

A meeting of supporters of the Supreme Soviet, for which official permission had been granted by the Moscow Soviet, met from the start with resistance from the militia. Members of the militia in helmets, and with shields and clubs, tried to force demonstrators and mere onlookers away from the square. In response, the demonstrators began building barricades.

In order to keep the demonstrators from consolidating their hold on the square, an OMON detachment emerged from the militia ranks and began clubbing people near the barricade. This time, however, the OMON met with an unexpected rebuff. Making use of materials from nearby building sites, some of the demonstrators armed themselves with stones, boards, and pieces of metal, and began to fight the OMON. There were serious casualties on both sides. Despite using tear gas and rubber bullets, the OMON were forced to retreat.

The militia tried several times, unsuccessfully, to storm the barricade, which the demonstrators had set on fire. To keep events from developing in a dangerous direction, Chairperson of the Moscow Soviet Nikolay Gonchar came to the square and began talking to the demonstrators and to the forces surrounding the square. Thanks to his efforts as a mediator, the defenders of the barricade handed over several bottles of gasoline. The militia and the demonstrators finally dispersed from Smolenskaya Square without further clashes.

This time, thanks largely to Gonchar, the flames of confrontation were put out. But not, unfortunately, for long.

From Kaluzhskaya Square to the House of Soviets

The meeting called by the Front for National Salvation for Kaluzhskaya Square at 2 p.m. on October 3 also had official permission. But militia forces blocked the exits from the nearest metro stations and all the streets leading onto the square, and told the people who came to take part that it had been banned. No one attempted to break through this cordon. After some time, the militia themselves opened the way for the demonstrators onto the Krymskiy Embankment, but at the Krymskiy Bridge, rows of soldiers from the Interior Ministry forces blocked the route.

After several days of clashes around the House of Soviets, and following the events on Smolenskaya Square, the demonstrators were in a determined mood. On this day, for the first time, it was not the militia and OMON that attacked the demonstrators, but the demonstrators that set out to break through the cordon. Eyewitness testimonies can best describe what happened after that.

However, we feel it is necessary to pose a whole series of questions which need to be clarified.

Why were only very small forces from the Interior Ministry, insufficient to hold back the demonstrators, placed on the demonstrators' route to the House of Soviets?

The Interior Ministry had considerable forces at its disposal—the Dzershinskiy Division of troops, the Moscow OMON, the Moscow militia, OMON detachments brought into Moscow from other regions of Russia, and cadets from several Interior Ministry training colleges. Nothing explains the dispersal of forces in several directions, and their concentration mainly at the House of Soviets. At the House of Soviets, meanwhile, there was practically no resistance; the forces imposing the blockade quit their positions and departed.

Some suggest that the Interior Ministry forces simply did not expect such a large number of demonstrators and such vigorous attacks. They became confused, succumbed to panic, and failed to block the way of the demonstrators in an organized manner. This is partly correct. But there is reason to suppose that the panic and confusion stemmed not only from the actions of the demonstrators, but also from the orders issued by the Interior Ministry chiefs. Large militia forces were quickly concentrated in the path of the demonstrators in the vicinity of Smolenskaya Square. We ourselves saw large numbers of trucks and buses full of militia members. But members of the militia and the Interior Ministry staff informed us privately that they were ordered to retreat—in the very minutes when the demonstrators were approaching. Transcripts of radio conversations confirm this. Many trucks and buses were already surrounded by demonstrators, and this departure on command turned into panic-stricken flight. Why was this order given?

Usually, when they want to block demonstrators' path, the Moscow militia set up barriers consisting of one or two rows of heavy trucks. Demonstrators have never succeeded in breaking through such a barrier, especially if it has been reinforced with lines of militia members. Even in the fierce clash on May 1, 1993, the demonstrators did not succeed in forcing their way through the barrier that was set up literally in front of their eyes. On October 3 there was no attempt to set up such a barrier, despite the fact that dozens of trucks had earlier been concentrated in the path of the demonstrators. Why?

Two explanations are possible.

The first is that the militia leaders were wavering, were unsure of the outcome of the political conflict, and feared that the scales would come down on the side of the Supreme Soviet. From this stemmed their indecisiveness and their contradictory actions.

The second possible explanation is that the Interior Ministry chiefs simply had no wish to block the demonstrators. Their intention was to draw the demonstrators into skirmishes with small militia forces, to allow the logic of the development of these clashes to turn the demonstrators into an uncontrolled mob, and then, under the pretext of defending the population against mass disorders, to use harsh methods to crush the opposition.

It is now difficult to draw a clear conclusion. It is possible, however, that there is an element of truth in each of these explanations.

A.I. Kolganov
EYEWITNESS TESTIMONY
(continued)

The demonstration on October 3. On Soviet Square, the meeting set for 1 p.m. failed to materialize. There were no more than a hundred people and a few buses full of OMON. I set off for Kaluzhskaya (Oktyabrskaya) Square, where a demonstration was scheduled for 2 p.m. Here I saw large forces of militia—all in helmets and bulletproof vests, and with shields and clubs. Most of them, or a very significant part, had officers' epaulettes.

A line of militia stood in front of the exit from the radial metro station, and also in front of the entrance. We evaded the cordon by going across a garden. Yet another militia line blocked our path. We outflanked this as well by going along a carriage path, and headed for the monument in the middle of the square. Here there was no cordon; the militia stood in groups and hunted away people who penetrated there from time to time. At the circle line metro station there were noticeably more people, but a militia cordon was holding them back as well. We could also see a large crowd of people at the beginning of Leninskiy Prospekt: a line of militia was standing there, too.

Suddenly, we heard a shout. A large crowd of people with banners and signs flooded onto the square, and then turned into the Krymskiy Embankment. When they reached the bridge, they halted. The way ahead of them was blocked by what appeared to be two lines (perhaps more, but it was difficult to tell, since they were standing higher up on the bridge) of Interior Ministry troops, mainly youths of eighteen or nineteen. The demonstrators numbered at least ten thousand.

A short distance ahead of the main mass of people, a vanguard of three or four hundred demonstrators approached the soldiers. In the first rows of this vanguard, forty to sixty people marched with the air of militants. For the most part, these were men between twenty-five and forty. Some had covered their faces with scarves. Someone gave the command from within their ranks: "Slowly, start moving forward slowly!" The front ranks of the demonstrators reached the line of troops. Clubs appeared for an instant. Several chunks of asphalt flew through the air from the demonstrators' side.

The soldiers' formation was broken quickly. The crowd swept around them and carried them along. Some of the soldiers climbed off the bridge by the side staircases. The most aggressive demonstrators tried to beat up the remaining soldiers. I helped other demonstrators drag soldiers aside, giving them the chance to leave the scene. A group of demonstrators carried a wounded soldier past me; there was blood on the side of his bulletproof vest. Only once did I see an Interior Ministry soldier helping demonstrators carry off another soldier: only demonstrators helped the other wounded and injured troops. Under his military jacket, one of the wounded was wearing a militia uniform—it was impossible to tell what forces our opponents were from.

At the Park Kultury metro station, Interior Ministry troops again formed up in lines across the road, but these lines were also quickly broken. On the way to Zubovskaya Square, the demonstrators seized a truck belonging to the militia or to an Interior Ministry unit; it had been abandoned with the keys still in the ignition. There were many trucks standing alongside the Garden Ring Road. The militia did not attempt to use them to create barriers, as they had done repeatedly in other places. There were enough trucks to ensure that such a barrier would have been practically insurmountable, but it wasn't done. Not a single OMON member was visible; they had been at Sovietskaya Square, but not at Kaluzhskaya Square. Where had they all suddenly disappeared to? Only a few young men from the Interior Ministry forces and small groups of militia were in sight.

Just behind Smolenskaya Square, the militia made another attempt to form up in lines. The day was sunny, and the shields were gleaming. Once again the demonstrators broke their lines. The militia and internal troops had three fire trucks there, and now they brought one into action. The demonstrators fled to the sides of the street to avoid the jet of foam, but did not turn back. They threw stones at the windows of the fire trucks, which were protected by metal grilles, and beat on the trucks with boards. The trucks maneuvered wildly and dangerously, trying to escape the skirmish.

The other vehicles that were present—ordinary trucks and buses, and special militia vehicles—were driven in just as wild and dangerous a fashion. In some of them were militia members. Demonstrators flung stones at the vehicles. The militia members who were in the trucks and buses jumped out of them and fled. One of the vehicles, a GAZ-66 van, rammed another GAZ-66 while executing violent maneuvers in an effort to turn around and get away. At precisely that moment, people in militia uniform, with helmets, bulletproof vests, and shields, leapt from the first van. One of them was struck by the side of his own van, as it was thrust suddenly aside by the impact of the other vehicle. He fell to the ground, and lay on his side. His comrades abandoned him, and a group of demonstrators tried to provide him with help.

Several times, the militia fired tear gas canisters into the crowd of demonstrators. But there were so few of these canisters that they merely served to irritate people. Again, the militia made no attempt to set up a barrier of trucks, though dozens of trucks were present. Demonstrators threw stones and boards flew after the retreating Interior Ministry troops. Some equipped themselves with aluminium shields seized from their adversaries, and they captured three more trucks.

The demonstrators in the front ranks were shouting constantly, calling on those further back to catch up. They were alarmed by the way the column was becoming strung out; they were afraid that the militia or the OMON would attack from side streets and divide the marchers into several sections. But nothing of the sort was tried. Ultimately, there were not even any attempts to defend the barriers at the House of Soviets. The forces that had made up the cordon retreated to the mayor's office and onto the bridge. Deputy of the Russian Federation Konstantinov tried to reason with an over-aggressive demonstrator, impressing on him that there was no point in provoking a clash with the forces guarding the mayor's office.

The trucks that the demonstrators had seized dragged away several street-cleaning vehicles and coils of razor wire without encountering any opposition. The demonstrators advanced toward the House of Soviets. A small group of demonstrators approached the cordon around the mayor's office, the former building of the Council for Mutual Economic Assistance. A single shot rang out. One of the demonstrators, an elderly man, fell to the ground, possibly hit by a rubber bullet. Two militia members ran up to him from the cordon, and dragged him across the lawn toward the mayor's office. Several demonstrators ran towards them. A scuffle ensued, involving mainly fists.... At that moment, a burst of automatic rifle fire rang out, then more and more bursts.

When I heard the first shots, I threw myself flat on the ground. I glanced around quickly. The demonstrators were fleeing. A few had taken cover behind the granite-clad entrance ramp of the mayor's office. Two or three soldiers had run forward, and one was even behind my back. They were firing their rifles from the hip, without taking aim. There was no whistle of bullets, and I could not see where bullets were striking. I began to think they were probably firing blanks, but later I heard reports that several demonstrators had received gunshot wounds. Unfortunately, I did not think to pick up the spent cartridges.

The shooting quickly died away (in all there were fifteen to twenty bursts of firing, mainly long ones). Only a few people had been shooting, perhaps three or five. The crowd regained its composure, and again headed toward the House of Soviets. I got up and left. Demonstrators streamed past me in disorderly groups. A bus drove up, carrying about fifty militia members with automatic rifles: they got out, stood for a while on the sidewalk, then piled back into the bus and drove off. At 3:30 p.m., I phoned home from the intersection of the New Arbat and the Garden Ring Road: "I'm alive. I'm heading home. All hell's going to break loose here." I can't say I was particularly afraid when I heard the bursts of automatic fire, but now I found the situation really terrifying. On both sides, nerves were at breaking point. I was scared that any provocation could result in a clash far bloodier than any up to that point.

(Manuscript testimony)

Testimony of V.S. Savelev:

On October 3, I was on Oktyabrskaya Square with the Voloshin medical brigade, which contains people with left-wing views, and also members of Memorial. We were observing the famous demonstration. The square was surrounded with militia detachments, equipped mainly with shields and clubs—there were practically no firearms. The militia were packed so tightly together that the demonstrators, who numbered about fifteen thousand, couldn't get past them. The only outlet from Kaluzhskaya Square that was left open for the demonstration was the road leading to the Krymskiy Bridge.

We were watching the demonstration from the side, from a hundred meters off, and saw how the demonstrators were forced to turn toward the Krymskiy Bridge. Then we went between the buildings, and from beside the bridge we saw how a small, thin line of OMON members had been placed in the middle of the bridge. The OMON tried to stop the column of demonstrators with their clubs. The demonstrators replied with stones. We saw how shields and helmets that had been taken from the OMON were thrown into the Moscow River, and then how OMON troops fled down the staircases at the side of the bridge. Already worked up, the demonstrators threw stones at them. We gave first aid to several OMON members and a number of demonstrators. The demonstrators included many elderly people. I remember an old woman whose arms had been beaten.

After this, the demonstration turned into a mob and went out of control. When we followed after the demonstrators, we saw firefighters with flamethrowers which had evidently been used to try to disperse the demonstration. One of the firefighters had a head wound. We also saw buses full of OMON troops standing to one side. Young people from among the demonstrators, thirty or forty of them, were standing with arms linked and allowing the OMON members to leave—they were running off into gateways. Opposite them stood twenty old people, crowded together, shouting at them angrily.

The demonstrators seized a number of trucks which had been abandoned along with their ignition keys. The trucks were immediately started up, demonstrators climbed in, and they drove off to try to break through to the White House. The siege was lifted, and thousands of people, perhaps fifteen to twenty thousand, stood around the White House.

After this we heard that the command had been given to seize the mayor's office.

(Testimony tape-recorded by Andrei Kolganov)

Interview with A.V. Kryuchkov (obtained by A.V. Buzgalin):
Anatoliy Viktorovich, what happened after the demonstrators broke through to the House of Soviets?
I'd do better to take events in order, from the beginning.
The march on October 3 began at Oktyabrskaya Square and headed toward the House of Soviets, though the original plan was to head along Leninskiy Prospekt. There were several cordons, perhaps six rows of militia and OMON troops. The first cordons were relatively tough.
These were made up of OMON troops? I had the impression that they were new recruits.
No, not all of them were new recruits. There were Interior Ministry troops, but there were also OMON members. Of course, there weren't very many of them—I'll explain why later.
There were three rows of them on the Krymskiy Bridge?
More than that. In the first cordon there were four or five rows. I was on the left flank, going away from Oktyabrskaya Square, and I tried to do some agitating among them.
How did the breakthrough occur? Did someone attack the cordon, or did you simply start forcing them out of the way?
At first we stopped. I told Urazhtsev that it was necessary to try to talk to them first. We had to try to convince them to stand aside, to let people through, and we should only take other measures if this failed. We talked to them for ten or fifteen minutes. I was on the left flank, and Urazhtsev and Bratishchev on the right. We explained the situation, telling them why Yeltsin was no longer the lawful president, and why they were obliged to carry out the instructions of another minister—we read out the appropriate order. We asked them to allow us to exercise our democratic rights, to go through to the House of Soviets and express our views on what was happening.
Then we warned them that if they didn't make way for peaceful demonstrators who weren't looking for a fight with them, they would become accomplices in a crime. After this, the column moved toward us. The demonstrators made no attempt to strike any blows. When the

lines met, the militia, as usual, began beating the demonstrators with their clubs. The breakthrough took place simply through force of numbers, through mass pressure. Finally, when the militia began clubbing people, the demonstrators began tearing away their shields and clubs, and a brawl took place.

With the next cordon it was much the same. I went out in front, and again warned them of their responsibility and called on them to step aside, but the dialogue was very brief because the crowd was already catching up. These cordons had vehicles. At the second cordon they were already using gas—they were firing gas canisters. Then there was a cordon with a row of vehicles—street-cleaning vehicles and trucks.

But they didn't manage to block the road, or make it seem that they were blocking it?

My guess is that they simply weren't ready. They didn't know where the main blow, so to speak, was going to come, where the main forces were heading. When we worked out our plan of action, this is what we had in mind—we were going to force them to run from one end of Moscow to the other. Demonstrations were to be held not only on Oktyabrskaya Square, but also on Sovetskaya Square, on Ilich Square, at the Belorusskiy train station, and at the Barrikadnaya metro. So the militia were forced to prepare for marches coming from various directions, keeping their forces in various places, and concentrating most of their strength at the House of Soviets. This is why they didn't manage to block our path. In addition to that, they were suffering from a certain amount of confusion. I have the impression that they simply weren't expecting so many people.

When the demonstrators were approaching the White House, shots began to be fired over their heads. Were these blank rounds or not?

Here I can't begin to judge. I was concentrating entirely on evaluating the situation. The question I was interested in above all was whether it was possible to break the blockade on the House of Soviets. As well as that, I was scared that the column might be divided up, that there would be attempts to cut off its first section. Such an attempt was in fact made at the beginning of the march. Of course, I heard the shots, but I couldn't tell what they were shooting.

Breaking the blockade turned out to be quite simple. When we were approaching the House of Soviets, it was clear that the cordon was already very weak, and that in some places it had completely disappeared. There was a barrier of vehicles, street-cleaning vehicles and trucks, with thirty or forty militia members in front of them and about the same number behind. But when the militia saw that groups of defenders of the House of Soviets were approaching them from behind, they became scared of being caught in a trap, and began to scatter. So there were no clashes in front of this last cordon. The two or three remaining soldiers didn't try to stop us penetrating the cordon.

3
BLOOD

After breaking the blockade around the House of Soviets, the demonstrators clashed with the militia and internal troops near the mayor's office and the Hotel Mir. Around the same time, Rutskoi issued an order to storm the mayor's office and the Ostankino television center. All blockade forces had already begun to retreat. Around 4 p.m., Yeltsin proclaimed a state of emergency in Moscow. In his decree, he characterized the supporters of the opposition as bandits attacking peaceful citizens.

From 6 p.m. on, the opposition demonstrators—around four thousand people—were concentrated near the Ostankino television center. Most were unarmed and had come on foot. A small armed group without heavy weapons arrived by truck; estimates range from twenty to a hundred people. About five hundred members of the Vityaz special forces detachment and twenty-one OMON armored carriers with heavy machine guns defended the large Ostankino television complex.

Under very unclear circumstances, the offensive side made one shot from an anti-tank grenade gun. Immediately afterwards, the defenders opened fire, first from one of the buildings and then from the other. Then the armored carriers opened heavy machine-gun fire. In the open square in front of the television center, more than fifty unarmed demonstrators were killed and dozens were wounded. One soldier was killed.

STORMING THE MAYOR'S OFFICE

The circumstances surrounding the storming of the mayor's office are still unclear. There was shooting, but who fired the shots? From which side? Each side accuses the other. Were there casualties? Probably yes, but both sides say the dead were from their side. How many victims were there? On the side of the militia, no more than two people. The Chief Administration of Internal Affairs of Moscow reported that two people were killed on October 3, up until the time of the attack on the television center. One of these two, however, was the militia officer killed in the truck collision while the demonstrators were breaking through militia lines on the Garden Ring Road, hours before the attack on the mayor's office.

The call for the storming of the mayor's office, and simultaneously, for the attack on the Ostankino Television Center, came from Rutskoi, speaking to the thousands of people who had just broken through the blockade on the House of Soviets. But even before this, many demonstrators had called for seizing the mayor's office, which the commanders of the militia and internal troops were using as a temporary headquarters. Yuriy Luzhkov, the mayor, was also an open supporter of the use of force against the Supreme Soviet.

The attack on the mayor's office was the opposition leaders' first step in a transition from defending the constitution and the rule of law to using force in order to struggle for power. It was also the first step on their road to defeat. Up to this point, they had been able to resist Yeltsin's pressure thanks only to their moral authority. Their position as the defenders of the law and the constitution—persecuted; blockaded in the House of Soviets

The Hotel Mir—the "Peace" Hotel—near the White House and the mayor's office, just after 5 p.m. on October 4. Sniper fire came from this direction beginning on October 3 and continuing even after the surrender, which occurred around 4 p.m. on October 4, as unarmed people were attempting to leave the White House.

[Photo by Vojtech Lavicka]

without telephone service, electricity, water, or heat; beaten up on the streets and squares of Moscow by the militia and the OMON—had increased this moral authority with every day that passed.

As explained earlier, neither Yeltsin nor the Supreme Soviet enjoyed real mass support during these September and October days. Thus, chance events could easily change the balance of forces, giving a small advantage to one side or the other. Such small advantages could determine the outcome of the struggle. On October 3, the balance was shifting to the advantage of the Supreme Soviet. The army and the security forces, despite retaining their loyalty to Yeltsin, were unreliable. Even their leaders were declaring that they would not meddle in a political conflict. Only the less powerful, less well trained Interior Ministry forces were solidly behind the president. Finally, most of the regional elites had come out in favor of the zero option.

Yeltsin was wavering. Reports were appearing in newspapers to the effect that he was ready to agree to simultaneous early elections for the president and parliament (after the October events, Yeltsin denied these reports). Direct talks between representatives of the president and the Supreme Soviet had begun, mediated by the Patriarch of Moscow and of all Russia Aleksiy II. After the demonstrators broke through the blockade on the House of Soviets, even the pro-Yeltsin television changed the way it presented reports. The usual scornful commentaries on the opposition disappeared from the broadcasts.

Then came the attack on the mayor's office. Why?

A multitude of factors seem to have influenced this decision. The many days of inactivity while under siege, and the sleepless nights while awaiting a nighttime assault, all raised the level of nervous tension—on the part of all the Parliament defenders, from the top command to the rank and file—to breaking point. The sudden lifting of the blockade, creating the possibility of action, led to a purely emotional outburst—to a decision, which must have seemed easy and obvious, to deal first of all with the immediate threat to the House of Soviets posed by the forces concentrated in the mayor's office. The political significance of this step was not thought through, even though many of the people around Rutskoi who were able to make a more considered estimate of the situation protested the decision openly. Perhaps Rutskoi and others perceived ten or fifteen thousand demonstrators forcing aside the cordon surrounding the House of Soviets as a general popular uprising against Yeltsin, wanted to believe that this was the case, and acted under the influence of this clearly exaggerated assessment.

The provocative behavior of the Interior Ministry forces, who for several days had been inflaming the situation with their vicious attacks on demonstrators and on any small group of people that approached their cordons, also undoubtedly played a role. When shots were fired on demonstrators from the direction of the mayor's office, it was the last straw. The crowd was becoming ungovernable. This, too, may have helped goad Rutskoi to make his impetuous call. Not wanting the crowd to begin acting on its own initiative, he tried to retain at least the appearance of control. It was precisely this step, however, which signified that control had been irretrievably lost. From then on, events developed irrespective of the wishes of Rutskoi or of anyone else from the leadership of the Supreme Soviet.

It should be noted that the store of weapons that television reporters discovered in the mayor's office showed clearly that the forces located there had been intended for use in storming the House of Soviets. Some of this weaponry was shown on television; it included heavy-caliber machine guns, grenade launchers, and even flamethrowers. It was quite obvious that neither grenade launchers nor flamethrowers were needed to carry out the officially proclaimed task of preventing the distribution of weapons from the House of Soviets. Nor was there any need for armored vehicles, more than ten of them, equipped with heavy weapons.

Interview with Anatoliy Kryuchkov (obtained by Alexander Buzgalin)

How did the spontaneous meeting in front of the House of Soviets come about, and what exactly did Rutskoi say? Did the idea of going to Ostankino come from him, or did it arise in some other fashion?

Since I was responsible for organizing the meeting, I thought it was essential for people to study the situation and work out what steps needed to be taken. I finished installing microphones for the meeting, and asked that the speakers be found—most of them were people's deputies. Rutskoi appeared soon after I opened the meeting, probably about ten minutes late. He had not had the chance to discuss his decision with other representatives of the opposition, since on October 3 most of the leaders were outside the House of Soviets. Everything happened very quickly. It struck me that Rutskoi had taken the decision spontaneously, under the direct influence of the situation that had arisen. I found his decision to call for the storming of the mayor's office and Ostankino rather unexpected, especially the second part. When he finished making his appeal I suggested another option to him, but he wouldn't listen to me. I had the impression that he'd taken this decision independently. During the previous three days there had been no more than a thousand people in the House of Soviets, and when we brought a crowd of many thousands, it seemed to him that with this support he could solve any problem. I can understand the psychology of it. He'd become psychologically unstable, and when he had to make decisions in an extreme situation that he thought was a winning one, he made a stupid choice without considering the consequences.

When the attack took place on the mayor's office, were any provocative shots fired?

While these events were taking place I was in the House of Soviets, trying to resolve various questions (this had to do with the proposals I'd made to Rutskoi, and which he hadn't listened to, but which I still tried to put into effect...). I can only relay the words of people who were eyewitnesses. My comrades who were present state that no order to fire was given from our side. Also, one of the members of the Political Council of our party, who was there, witnessed the following scene. When people began firing from a rooftop on the defenders of the mayor's office, that is, on members of the militia, one of their commanders, looking at the roof of the building from which fire was being directed at his fellow militia, began shouting into a portable radio: "What are you shooting at your own people for? I'll take you down off the roof if you continue shooting at us!" Not just one of my comrades, but another as well witnessed this.

From this, I conclude that it was the other side that provoked the shooting. Eyewitnesses from our side (I only have access to these testimonies) state that when they moved toward the mayor's office, the crowd was made up essentially of the same people that we'd led to the House of Soviets. Earlier, I'd been marching in the middle or the front of the column, and I hadn't seen anyone with any kind of firearm. At most they had shields and clubs which they'd taken from the militia. I didn't see anyone with a rifle or pistol. The soldiers and members of the volunteer corps who were inside the White House and had weapons were supposed to stay inside and guard the command posts. According to my information, they didn't join the move on the mayor's office. So in fact, our side didn't have anything to shoot with. It's possible that someone who was supposed to be in the House of Soviets set off for the mayor's office carrying a gun, but I can't agree with the argument the democrats are trying to put across: that this was a powerful assault group with a large number of firearms, and that they burst through the defenses of the mayor's office using their weapons. According to my information, the only significant act of violence was the use of a truck to smash through the glass in the building. One of the trucks that had been abandoned at the mayor's office was driven onto the upper level and used to ram the glass so that people could get inside.

(Tape recording)

Testimony of Vladimir Savelev (continued):

The OMON and militia retreated into various streets next to the White House and the mayor's office without putting up any resistance. One group of the OMON barricaded themselves under the entrance bridge at the mayor's office. When I approached them and asked if there were any injured, they replied that there were none. After this, the order was given to seize the mayor's office. While this was underway, we heard shooting, and people left the mayor's office. After five or ten minutes, down below at the mayor's office, a detachment of somewhere between fifty and a hundred OMON members smashed the windows from the inside, and came out. They lined up and headed off from the mayor's office at a run.

(Testimony recorded by Andrei Kolganov)

Sebastian Job
VICTORY AND DEFEAT OF THE RUSSIAN WHITE HOUSE: ASSESSMENT OF AN EYEWITNESS

....The crowd turns the corner, left into Kalinin Prospekt (the New Arbat). From here, it is a clear run down to the White House.

The final hurdle is easily passed. The thin cordon at the entrance to the grounds barely puts up any fight. I wait a second as the razor wire is cut and dragged. Some people's hands are bleeding. There are shouts of "Careful!" I jump where the wire is flattest, and I am in.

Just in front of me an officer walks up a driveway ramp and starts to argue with the demonstrators. I can't hear what he is saying because of the repeated screaming of the man next to me: "Get out of here!" he rages at the officer, as if trying to save his life. The officer doesn't move. My neighbor throws a bent steel tool, which hits him on the arm. For a moment the stern look on his face doesn't change—then he grimaces, and clutches at the point of impact. He is wearing a heavy wool coat, but obviously it hurts a lot. He turns and walks away.

I climb onto the curved ramp which the officer has abandoned. Triumphant shouts and laughter echo off the buildings. It is incredible. In all the scenarios I had imagined and discussed for the resolution of this crisis, it had never once come to me that the blockade might be broken by civilians, massed and determined.

Two or three loud reports. Shots? I crouch down a little. Everywhere there is a nervous silence. Next I am flat on my stomach, watching as a soldier about twenty meters further up the ramp fires a machine gun toward the crowd below. Is he firing at the people, or a little above them? I can't tell.

They will later be swamped by much worse, but these are the first bullets. They make a searing and shocking sound. The violence of the last hours, often disgusting, had a rough justice. The street fighting involved risk for all, and retained a sort of human quality, or perhaps just animal ferocity. This firing on civilians is machinic, removed, and lethal.

I dive over a retaining wall and take shelter under the ramp. From here, I watch as the soldier sprays the area until his cartridge is empty. Then he walks rapidly up the ramp toward the green skyscraper from which he must have come. The mayor's office is the former COMECON building (COMECON was the Soviet bloc's trading organization); a nice piece of real estate hastily expropriated after the August 1991 coup by the previous mayor, Gavriil Popov. More recently it has been a command post for the blockade. The soldier seems to be warning: you can take back the parliament, but this here is ours.

....I hear shooting near the mayor's building. People are running away. I mount the stairs to the elevated tarmac, and watch from behind an empty sentry box as five or six young men exchange machine gun fire with others I can't see. I gather from their simple khaki uniforms that they are from the parliament guard.

One of them backs an army truck at high speed into the double glass doors of the entrance. He keeps doing this until someone shoots out his gas tank and one of his tires. Just below me, there comes a huge crash. Another truck is smashing through a ground floor entrance. Naively, I imagine that this is pointless vandalism, and wonder when they will be reined in.

Reality is more ominous. The mayor's building is being invaded. The civilian phase is giving way to the military phase. Liberation has become offensive.

This is the first of many fatal steps. Is it really necessary? Is this building needed for defense? Might Yeltsin be dissuaded from attack? Might he be forced into genuine negotiations if the protesters simply reclaim the parliament, proclaim it alive again? I can't say, and the chance to find out is being lost.

I follow the parliament soldiers through the smashed-in doors. The building seems to be falling without a struggle. A crowd of protesters and journalists presses tight into this dangerous space of falling glass and gas fumes. A corridor of people is formed and seven or eight captives are marched out, some looking roughed up. A man comes through proudly holding a tin box. He rattles a great circle of keys: "From the mayor's desk!" he shouts.

The word "Ostankino" is on everybody's lips....

(Manuscript testimony)

Story of a depoliticized militia officer (recorded by Nadezhda Bondarenko):

I work in an ordinary militia station, a long way from the center of town. At the time of all these events ... not a single person was sent to us from the White House. In our militia district there wasn't a single person arrested for political reasons. And here they were sending us to the White House. No one explained anything, no one told us which side we were supposed to fight on, or why.... You see, the militia are now depoliticized, so no one explains anything to us about political events. Even among ourselves, we no longer talk freely about what we think. When all this began ... the abolition of the parliament, no one in the station said who they supported, everyone kept silent. Basically, we were just put next to the White House and told to maintain order....

When the shooting began, everything was unclear—who was shooting, from which side, and why.... We were shooting too. Personally I couldn't fire on people, and neither could a lot of our people—we just fired at random.... I hope very much that we didn't kill anyone. There were people who didn't take their weapons out at all.

Meanwhile, three of my comrades were killed, and one very severely wounded. I don't even know who was shooting at them— whether it was democrats, communists, or someone else.... It's a terrible thing, when in front of your eyes, someone you've worked with for many years....

Then the people in the White House seized us as hostages. And the way they treated us was far from the best. One man, in civilian clothes but armed with an automatic rifle, was bawling out that we were traitors to our homeland, and threatened to shoot us all unless we immediately came over to the side of the Supreme Soviet. All the same, we refused. How can I choose sides, if I don't know who's in the right, and who's guilty?... Naturally, they took our weapons. But they guarded us badly— we managed to flee.

Now they've given us a bonus, eighty thousand rubles each. No one's refused it, everyone's taken it, you know what life's like now— without money you're helpless.... But the people from the department for the struggle against organized crime got a lot more, and they also received really good winter uniforms, the kind we wouldn't even dream of. And they'll tell you themselves that they were sitting in their barracks, didn't even go out. While we were out there in the rain and snow....

Of course, eighty thousand is still money.... But my three comrades who were killed don't need a bonus any more. And a fourth is lying with a bullet wound in his lungs, it's not yet clear whether he's going to live.... He's such a great guy! And those three were also good guys.... But you can't tell that to the people who fought for the Supreme Soviet! They're mourning their own dead now—they don't care about ours! And the government has simply loaded the blame onto us.

What? You're asking whether anyone took to drinking after these events?... We were drinking while the events were going on. Every day, as long as it lasted. We drank to get warm, and simply for the sake of drinking. None of our commanders even mentioned this, and no one stopped us....

N. N., member of a fighting detachment
TWELVE DAYS OF CRISIS

There was a roar of voices, and people were running around. Everyone rushed to the windows. A crowd with red flags was coming along the Arbat. Those were our people! They'd broken through!... From the Arbat we could hear shouts, and the bursting of gas grenades. Two lines of people with helmets and shields were formed up diagonally from the mayor's office to us.... On the Arbat (we couldn't see this because of a garden) there was obviously a ferocious battle going on. Tear gas hung in the air. Shots could be heard—single rounds, and bursts of automatic fire. Were these gas canisters? Blanks? Then suddenly the rows of OMON broke up, the crowd surged past the mayor's office, and a colorful array of flags, signs, and happy, excited people rushed around the forecourt of the House of Soviets.

Our battalion commander shouted from behind: "Hold your positions! Don't go beyond the barricade! Don't throw stones!" Damned discipline. In front of us, at the Hotel Mir, a skirmish was in progress. The line of helmets broke; some of these troops retreated onto the ramp of the mayor's office, and the rest tried to defend themselves in front of the hotel. Their shields were being ripped off them. The Yellow Goebbels, after bellowing at unbelievable volume, sped off in the direction of the Barrikadnaya metro station. An armored personnel carrier rolled forward into the crowd, and suddenly froze at an angle. Demonstrators climbed onto it. No, these were no longer demonstrators—they were insurgents! Then the machine roared once again, turned around, and took off. The people who had managed to cling to it were covering the viewing slits. The OMON members pulled people off by their legs, and beat them with sticks. Suddenly, abrupt and close by, came the sound of automatic rifle fire. Everyone rolled like peas off the armorplate. A person was seized and beaten, but meanwhile the crowd continued to press forward. At that point the formation collapsed. The hirelings of Luzhkov, Borovoy, and Co. scattered desperately, throwing away their shields, helmets, and overcoats. The armored personnel carrier roared backwards, blazed up from an accurately thrown gasoline bomb, and after extinguishing the fire with a cloud of freon, sped off after its scattering army. The crowd rushed after it. Someone in epaulettes halted and fired a burst from an automatic rifle, a whole clip. I clearly saw people fall, but now not even tanks could have stopped the rolling human wave....

Another minute or two, and the entire square in front of us was swamped by insurgent Moscow. Shots rang out in the vestibule of the hotel, at the mayor's office. The central barricade was hurriedly dismantled, and the human stream completely inundated Free Russia Square....

Rutskoi's amplified voice thundered over the square, calling on people to go out and storm the mayor's office. The crowd seethed, a spasm passed through it, and a furious avalanche rolled forward. From the humpbacked bridge, we saw Rutskoi leap out of the entrance and run in the first rows of the assault column. With him were four or five members of his guard, with automatic rifles.

The OMON put up only a lackluster resistance, and they were dumbfounded by their defeat. Within a minute the crowd swarmed up the ramp and over the forecourt of the mayor's office. Single shots and short bursts of gunfire resounded, and suddenly powerful bass notes joined in; these were no longer from rifles. The people who had rushed onto the forecourt fell to the ground, or ran back. People lay down on the staircase, but then immediately leapt up and ran directly into the gunfire. There was a brief skirmish at the entrance, the sound of breaking glass, and then we watched as the crowd poured into the vestibule. Here was victory!

In the trucks of the OMON were abandoned items—clothing, ammunition, and radio transmitters. One truck stopped near our post, and we saw there several officers' overcoats (after the epaulettes and other insignia had been ripped off, the coats were given to the least well-clad of our fighters), and a pile of empty and partly empty vodka bottles. We summoned a photojournalist with a video camera and asked that this scene be recorded, so as to show who had really been drinking during the siege.

From the balcony of the Supreme Soviet it was announced that heavy-caliber machine guns and flamethrowers had been found in the building of the mayor's office. They had obviously been brought there for use on us.

(*Solidarnost*, no. 23, 1993)

SLAUGHTER AT OSTANKINO

The decision to organize an expedition to the Ostankino Television Center, in order to demand that the opposition be given the chance to put its case, was dictated more by the crowd than by political calculations. Like the storming of the mayor's office, the expedition to Ostankino signified a shift toward the use of violent methods to resolve the conflict. The attempt to use firearms to break into the building of the television center not only resulted in human casualties, but also served as a pretext for the subsequent tragic course of events, for the mass slaughter of the defenders of the House of Soviets.

Immediately after the bloody October events, some supporters of the opposition put forward the argument that everything which happened on October 3 and 4 was a planned provocation by the authorities. While we do not believe the attack on the television center was the direct result of provocation, it does seem clear that the authorities were content to allow the use of force to escalate.

We are certain that the actions of the authorities during the period from September 28 to October 3—above all, the constant unprovoked attacks by the militia and OMON on defenders of the Supreme Soviet, which were carried out with unprecedented ferocity—were aimed at goading the opposition into ill-considered responses. During the October 3 demonstration, sections of the militia and OMON forces were deliberately withdrawn from the path of the demonstrators. This can, of course, be explained by the confusion of the militia leadership. However, it is also possible that the authorities set out deliberately to give the supporters of the Supreme Soviet an exaggerated idea of their own strength, and to encourage them to underestimate the strength of the Yeltsin supporters. The aim, we believe, was to entice the leaders of the Supreme Soviet into a trap.

Among supporters of the radical opposition, Ostankino was a symbol of the ideological control the presidential authorities exercised over the population. Ostankino was described as the "empire of lies," and for some oppositionists, the urge to establish their own control over the television center became a virtual obsession. Oppositionists also remembered clearly the events of June 1992, when the OMON smashed a picket of the television center that had lasted many days, and beat the picketers savagely. At the time, the opposition press had emphasized the fact that the attack on the picket occurred at the same hour of the same day that the forces of Nazi Germany attacked the USSR in 1941—a day of national tragedy.

Reports that the television center was guarded only by small militia posts probably played a certain role. Indeed, only the usual groups of militia were on duty directly in front of the television center, and the only militia posts on the ground floor inside were the usual ones for the checking of passes. But hundreds of militia members and Interior Ministry troops were on the upper floors of the television center and in the surrounding area, along with several armored personnel carriers equipped with heavy-caliber machine guns, even though most of these forces were off to one side and had not taken up positions around the television center.

Centrists criticized Rutskoi's decision on political grounds. Radicals criticized it as bad military strategy. Both were ignored. Thousands of people flocked to Ostankino, which is in northern Moscow, about ten kilometers from the House of Soviets. A small number went to Ostankino in trucks and buses that had been captured during the storming of the mayor's office, including a group of between twenty and thirty armed people headed by General Makashov (the Interior Ministry later put the figure at a hundred). The rest went on foot, forming an impressive demonstration. Some used public transportation.

The Interior Ministry was aware of what the supporters of Rutskoi and the Supreme Soviet intended. As is shown by the transcripts of their radio conversations, including some that were included in television broadcasts, the Vityaz special forces detachment was ordered to follow directly behind the column of trucks and buses heading for the television center, but not to block its passage. Although the Interior Ministry had at its disposal massive forces that had been freed up once the cordon was withdrawn from around the House of Soviets, no attempts were made to stop supporters of Rutskoi from going to the television center. There were not even any attempts to block the movement of unarmed demonstrators, in order to spare them the dangers of a possible armed clash.

All these facts suggest that the forces supporting Yeltsin had considered in advance the possibility of a move on Ostankino, that they were monitoring the course of events, and that they had consciously prepared a trap at the television center for the supporters of the Supreme Soviet. They were not deterred by the likelihood of casualties; perhaps they even counted on casualties.

People began setting off for Ostankino at about 6 p.m., after the assault on the mayor's office. By 8 p.m. most of them had arrived at the television center and had assembled on the large square in front of it. Anpilov and Makashov were demanding that opposition political leaders be given the opportunity to address the population on television. The television center management rejected this demand. Demonstrators smashed the glass doors of the small building of the television center with a truck, and Rutskoi supporters entered the ground-floor vestibule. There, troops of the Vityaz detachment had already taken up positions. With the help of a megaphone, Anpilov and others called on them to lay down their weapons and to go over to the side of the Supreme Soviet.

After the blockade on the House of Soviets was broken, a Yeltsin decree imposed a state of emergency in Moscow from 4 p.m. on. This decree stipulated that if massive disorders broke out, and if anyone attempted to use firearms, troops were immediately to open fire. The chances that the standoff of armed people at the television center would be resolved peacefully were reduced almost to nil. Any gunshot, or any threatening move, could have irreparable consequences....

All of the eyewitnesses to the events agree that the exchange of fire broke out following a shot from a grenade launcher. The armed group of Rutskoi supporters had one grenade launcher and one grenade. How this happened is not clear. Rutskoi supporters argue that the grenade was launched unintentionally; according to their version, the first shot came from the building, the bullet struck the fighter who was holding the grenade launcher, and he involuntarily pulled the trigger.

Whatever the case, both sides opened fire. And from the first shot, troops opened fire from the upper floors of the small television center building onto the unarmed demonstrators on the square.

The armed group burst onto the ground floor of the main building. Despite the automatic fire, unarmed people followed them, pelting the area with stones. More effective were several gasoline bombs. At the base of the building, a fire blazed up and burned out three or four offices above the eastern entrance.

The forces were unequal, however, and within ten minutes the attackers were driven from the building. The shooting at unarmed demonstrators continued, first dying away and then intensifying. It was now crossfire from both buildings. There was almost nowhere to hide on the square; dead and wounded lay all over, and numerous volunteer medics dragged them out from under the bullets at the risk of their lives. Night fell, improving things at least a little for those who had been caught on the square by the shooting. Taking cover behind trucks and behind the trees growing here and there around the square, a few fighters tried to return the fire.

The stories told on television and radio, and repeated in Yeltsinist newspapers, that a full-scale battle took place inside the television center, that it was impossible to make television broadcasts, and that the center's personnel were forcibly evacuated, are pure inventions. Even if Ostankino had been stormed by a hundred armed fighters, they would not have been able to fully capture even half of one floor, let alone seize the colossal television and radio complex defended by hundreds of soldiers. In some television studios, where there was no order to evacuate, work continued on productions, and the people involved did not even suspect that a fire fight was under way on the square and in the first floor vestibule.

The head of the State Television and Radio Company, Vyacheslav Bragin, chose to cut off the television channels, even though the equipment of the smaller building, to which the attackers had not been able to penetrate, was at his disposal. His ban on handing out portable video cameras to television journalists and operators also seems strange. While the camera crews of foreign television companies were shooting the scene on the square, Russian television recorded nothing. The only scenes recorded inside the building were shot on the personal video camera of one of the workers. Bragin stated that he feared for the lives of his employees. It is true that some television journalists on the square were wounded, and that a French camera operator was killed.

One of the engineers of the television and radio complex was in fact killed by a stray bullet—it is not clear from which side. The fateful round from a grenade launcher that initiated the shooting killed a member of the Vityaz detachment. That was the sum total of the casualties among the defenders of the television center. Meanwhile, dozens of dead and wounded demonstrators lay on the square outside.

The 400 Interior Ministry troops and six armored personnel carriers at first took no part in what was occurring. They were later joined by a further 100 troops and fifteen armored personnel carriers. At about 10 p.m., several APCs approached the television center. One of them opened fire on the building with its heavy-caliber machine gun, then turned its turret and began firing on the demonstrators. The other APCs, turning on searchlights, conducted a thorough hunt for people trying to hide among the trees and bushes on the edge of the square and in the small groves adjoining it. Several more APCs opened fire along Korolev Street, which leads to the square.

The number of victims grew. Volunteers continued evacuating the wounded, transporting them in cars or abandoned trucks to the ambulances whose crews were reluctant to go nearer the scene because of the incessant gunfire. Toward midnight, the shooting almost died away. In the darkness, most of the demonstrators had succeeded in leaving the environs.

According to the official data, a total of sixty-six people were killed on October 3. Most of them were unarmed demonstrators cut down by machine-gun fire on the square in front of the television center. Major operations were performed on more than a hundred and fifty people with gunshot wounds.

It is hard to forget the last seconds recorded by the slain French camera operator. The darkness, illuminated by the flashes of gunshots, dissected by the searchlights of the armored personnel carriers and by lines of tracer bullets. The clear outline of the cement blocks with which the square was paved, and in the beams of the searchlights, corpses lying one on top of another. Then the camera jerked, and the image swung off to one side. The end....

But this was not yet the end. Maintaining their control of the mass media, Yeltsin's supporters spread a false account of the events at Ostankino. The events there were depicted as an extended battle inside the television center, lasting until midnight and with shifting fortunes. Needless to say, the shooting of unarmed people in crossfire on a square where there was no cover was not mentioned. An aggressive-minded crowd was reported to have taken part in an assault, and to have suffered in the course of a fire fight between armed Rutskoi supporters and the television center guards.

Laying all the responsibility for the bloodshed on the opposition, on Rutskoi and on the Supreme Soviet, Yeltsin and his confederates succeeded in forcing Defense Minister Pavel Grachev and the collegium of the defense ministry, after several hours of wavering, to give the order to bring army units into Moscow. They succeeded in finding several sections of elite military units which agreed to use force against the House of Soviets. The bloody denouement was approaching.

Testimony of Vladimir Savelev
(Recorded by Andrei Kolganov)

We then learned that the order had been given to storm Ostankino. We saw trucks and buses heading there. We collected bandages, and I agreed to go to Ostankino with the driver of a van. We took medical supplies from entrance twenty of the White House, where there was a first aid post. We discovered, incidentally, that the Moscow medical administration had refused to deliver supplies to the defenders of the White House even before this, and that they were extremely short of medicines and bandages.

At Ostankino there was a large crowd. We'd just caught up with the demonstration. There were a lot of young people there, and old ones as well. We had the feeling that they'd simply come to watch Ostankino pass into the hands of the opposition. We heard that talks had been going on there, but by the time we arrived it was already beginning to get dark, and it was obvious that something hadn't worked with the discussions. We heard a shot, probably from a grenade launcher—a very loud bang. Then there was a short exchange of gunfire. People were shouting that there were wounded. We had stretchers with us. We ran to the small Ostankino building, and helped load on a wounded man and carry him to the ambulance that was standing nearby.

After this, very intense shooting broke out. People began to flee and take cover. Very few of them had weapons. There was a sense that ten or perhaps fifteen automatic rifles were doing the shooting. The number of wounded increased, and we began taking them to the Sklifosovskiy Institute. The first person we took was dead on arrival. We were told that he was one of the people who had had rifles. The other people we took weren't opposition fighters. They were students, young guys who hadn't had firearms and who'd had no thought of using them. Most of them were people who'd been close to the television center and had been wounded by fire from inside. There was Vladimir Sychev, a photojournalist for a French agency, a biology student from Moscow State University, and several other people whose names I don't remember.

When we drove up to Ostankino again, constant firing was going on in short bursts. The firing seemed to be coming from all sides, it was impossible to tell from where, and tracer bullets were flying through the darkness. The people, who were mainly young, had taken cover around the fence that runs along Korolevskaya to the television tower. Then we saw an armored vehicle break through a barricade and drive up, with soldiers rushing behind it. I heard that the barricades had been erected on the orders of Konstantinov, who said that reinforcements were coming to help the troops defending Ostankino.

I had a red cross armband, and so they spared us. They already knew our vehicle. There was a constant, sparse firing —we had the feeling that people were shooting blindly at anything that moved. Toward nine or nine-thirty people began stopping us and asking us not to go up close, saying that the people in Ostankino were now firing on first aid teams. Two men in white coats then returned from helping someone, and they confirmed that people were coming under deliberate fire even when it was clear that they were wearing white coats. I was dressed in a light-colored raincoat, so they asked me not to go up close.

(Tape-recorded testimony)

Sebastian Job
VICTORY AND DEFEAT OF THE RUSSIAN WHITE HOUSE: ASSESSMENT OF AN EYEWITNESS

I arrive some time before seven o'clock. A crowd of a thousand people has broken the lock on the gate, and is sitting on the entrance steps to the main television building. Off to the right, beyond another fence, three armored personnel carriers sit quietly.

Viktor Anpilov, perhaps the most prominent of the Stalinist leaders, is there. He thinks the premises can be captured peacefully. "We are trying to convince the special troops, the Spetsnaz, not to fight.... They have taken off their masks, they have begun to talk to us. This is progress. So I cherish the hope that if the great mass of people come here, the soldiers will be with the people," he tells me. And Yeltsin's next move? "The next step of Yeltsin will be in the air to the United States of America," Anpilov chuckles.

More people are arriving but nothing seems to be happening except speeches. I go for a wander. I cross wide Korolevskaya, which bisects the complex, and begin to inspect the buildings on the other side. About two hundred meters up the road, outside the entrance to a smaller building, thirty or so demonstrators are standing silently at some portable barricades. About ten agitated soldiers are trying to keep them from coming closer. A small man with a moustache and a black beret is issuing orders. It is General Albert Makashov, one of Rutskoi's military command. I gather he has been unsuccessfully negotiating with the guard of the building.

Makashov takes the megaphone, points it at the building: "You have three minutes to come out." Silence. A captured army truck arrives. The barricades are opened and it drives head first into the metal and glass doors. This is done several times. The noise brings hundreds, and then perhaps thousands of people. They bunch in around the truck and the soldiers.

I have a choice position right by the doors, up on a double flower box. "Do you hear me? You have three minutes to leave, or we are coming in.... I give you my word that you will not be harmed," Makashov repeats. "What do you want?" I ask one of his gun-toting underlings, standing below me. "We are going to demand air time to address the people," he says. I have the feeling that Makashov's aims are not so modest.

A man kneels down in front of the truck and points a shoulder-mounted rocket launcher at the broken mouth of the entrance. By this time the number of armed people has risen to about thirty, and TV crews are illuminating the scene. The crowd starts chanting, "The enemies must leave!" psyching themselves up for the attack.

A single shot at very close range. Nobody moves. Slowly a thick-set man, armed, but not in uniform, slumps down against the wall across the entrance from me. No further shots follow. Medical people in white coats run in to help. Blood is coming from the man's right leg. Some of us argue about what has happened. Shot from the building? The angle would be very difficult. A pistol in his pocket accidentally discharged?

All questions are terminated by thunder from hell. An explosion. It throws me into the air. It kills I don't know how many others.

I find myself lying on the open footpath, under the street lamps. And then comes the shooting. From the second or third floor, not more than ten meters away, dozens of machine guns are pumping into the crowd. People must have run but I never saw them. There is no one around me. The semidarkness is cut by hundreds of deadly green tracer lines, shattered by unending noise. I crawl. A low wall traps me. I inch along its base, totally exposed, notice some people watching me from behind an orange water truck, notice my tape recorder, reach out a brainless hand and grab it, hold my bag between my head and the building, crawl. The air is bullets. Bullets and luck. For about thirty seconds of eternity I breathe luck, luck, luck. Wonderful luck brings the wall to an end, reveals the opening to an underground pedestrian crossing. I roll down the steps, roll into safety.

Down here there are twenty or so people. Two seem dead, a few are wounded, others are helping them. No one else gets in after me. "They shot at the people!" a man says to me. He can't believe it. I'm wondering about those still caught up there, meeting a fate determined by chance. I'm wondering about the woman with whom I shared the flower box.

The firing thins out. I make a run for it from the far end of the tunnel. I don't want to be here when the army arrives. Tunnels are like bridges.

From the end of the road I watch as the massacre evens out into a battle. A young crowd of mostly local people is standing about. We are not more than a few hundred meters away, but the shooting is across the road rather than along it. One man offers repeatedly to take me to his house to bandage my hand. It looks serious but it is not. I decide to be grateful: the wetness is freezing my hand in the cold night, and he has a telephone from which I can call in a report to the station.

Back at the end of the road, I get into a parked bus. It offers a front row view of the carnage, but my body and head are screaming at me to lie down. In the night's only compromise, I take a seat.

Five armored personnel carriers circle around without seeming to do very much. Molotov cocktails are thrown at the far corner of the building to keep it on fire, the shooting carries on, and brave people run out to drag back the fallen. The army has still not arrived....

....The spotlight of an armored personnel carrier falls on the bus. Suddenly it is spitting its fast green poison at us. We hit the floor, tumble out the door, run.

I stop behind a block of apartments. Like the explosion and initial machine gunning, this seems completely unwarranted. The carriers have patrolled right beside us half a dozen times. There are demonstrators among us, but like everyone in our area they are unarmed. Not a single provocation has come from this direction. A boy of seventeen is helped along past me. He has been shot in the head. His sister or girlfriend follows, her face too painful to describe.

I circle around the back of the burning building, cut through a forest to get a closer look. I come across people hiding behind trees, and a bunch of the afternoon's protesters using a shed for shelter. The high, bright moon also watches. And when soldiers are suddenly running our way, firing, hunting us in the forest, the watching moon becomes a dangerous spotlight, a participant, an enemy.

Interview with Anatoliy Kryuchkov (obtained by Alexander Buzgalin)

Could you tell us something about Ostankino, either from your own observations if you were there, or from the words of your comrades?

I wasn't at Ostankino for the simple reason that I was categorically opposed to storming the television center. I repeat: when I heard Rutskoi call for people to go to the mayor's office and Ostankino, I supported capturing the mayor's office, because that was the main source of pressure on the House of Soviets, that was the command post for the blockade on the House of Soviets, and the main forces were concentrated there. So I was in favor of that source being removed. But I was categorically opposed to storming Ostankino. I considered that even from a purely military point of view this was unrealistic, taking into account the strength we had at our disposal, the distance from where we were based, and several other factors. I couldn't go there both for this reason, and because from the political point of view I thought it was an adventure. So at this time I was elsewhere. After it had become clear that our suggestion wasn't being taken up, I decided that I'd try to carry it out independently anyway. There were reports that the General Staff, the headquarters of the Ministry of Defense, at the Arbatskaya metro station, was virtually undefended. I decided to check whether this was true, so I was there with a group of my comrades.

So once again, I can only talk about what happened at Ostankino on the basis of the testimonies of my comrades. From what they say, there was no order to use firearms either from Makashov or from Anpilov. Both Makashov and Anpilov called together the people who had guns (I can't say precisely how many they were, but according to the testimonies of our comrades it was a few dozen people), and the order was given not to use firearms. Makashov tried to set up talks. As people envisioned it, the task was simply to blockade the television center and to try to hold talks with the management in the hope of persuading them to give air time to our side. But then, seeing that these talks were fruitless because Bragin wouldn't come out to them—he sent a flat refusal through some of his co-workers—someone decided to ram the doors with a truck as had been done at the mayor's office, in order to break through to the inside. I don't know whether this was on Makashov's orders or independently—no one can give a precise answer on this point. According to our comrades, the first shots were fired from the side of the television center. As for the round from the grenade launcher, according to the testimony of eyewitnesses, the situation was like this: when the person who had the grenade launcher fell wounded, he fired the grenade off involuntarily. His finger was obviously on the trigger. So there was no command to open fire, and the goal wasn't to mount an assault as such on Ostankino, but to blockade the television center and to force its management to give air time to the defenders of the House of Soviets.

What were some of your other impressions of the night of October 3 and 4?

I have the impression that at 4 p.m. on October 3 our side had very good chances of success. I consider that this success, or to use a more grandiose term, victory, was let slip only because the people, the top people, in charge of the defense of the House of Soviets took stupid decisions. This was the case with the decision by Rutskoi. Also, there was a loss of tempo in this situation. The lines of communication of the defenders of the House of Soviets were stretched out. People were forced to scatter to various points of Moscow, trying to solve the problems involved in blockading the television center, or more precisely, of obtaining airtime. As a result of this loss of tempo, the scales started to swing gradually in the direction of our adversaries, and by somewhere around 11 p.m. I felt our chances of victory were gone. It was already clear that hopes of military units coming over to our side were unjustified.

Were there any reports of support from the armed forces or militia during the period from 3:30 in the afternoon of October 3 until the evening?

Yes, I was in Achalov's office when such a report came in. It was about 8 p.m., after I returned from the General Staff. Messages were said to have come from the Tulskaya parachute division and from the Tamanskaya division, saying that some subunits of these divisions had come over to our side and were on their way to assist us. But ultimately, these subunits didn't turn up, and how truthful the reports were, I don't know. I'm only talking about what I heard. Some other units were mentioned as well, but I was diverted at that point, because I was busy with my own tasks.

Report by Andrey Leybov in Echo-Conference SU.POL (fido.net), October 13, 1993

....According to Grachev, the guard at Ostankino consisted of about four hundred people and seven armored personnel carriers, while no more than about a hundred armed people came with Makashov. All attempts at storming the television center came to an end after the first ten minutes of the battle. What happened after that was the cold-blooded shooting of practically unarmed people by the APCs and by snipers. This is shown by the casualty figures. On the side of Ostankino four people died, while on the side of the opposition there were hundreds of dead and wounded (the total was drastically understated in the official figures).

Interview with Aleksandr Strakhov (Interviewer: Andrei Kolganov)

If we begin with the evening of October 3, I was struck by the psychosis that was built up in the course of the evening as the television channels shut down one after another. It was quite incomprehensible. Then a mobile studio appeared, and they began putting people into this studio in order to get their expressions of approval for what was happening. I recall at least two normal voices—I stress, not extreme, but normal. Those were the voices of Vladimir Yakovlevich Voroshilov, with whom I've had a long and close familiarity as a very stern, very judicious person. The second person, however strange it might seem, was Lenya Yarmolnik.

What they provided was simply a sober assessment of what happened. They didn't stick labels on anyone, but simply gave their views on what had happened. They said that you can't turn the country into an abattoir, you can't unleash a civil war, and that in their view everything hadn't been done, and still wasn't being done, to stop this happening. It struck me that these were sound comments. The tendentiousness of the mass media was obvious, and I didn't like it. I didn't like the form of presentation either. Unfortunately, most of the people who spoke were frothing at the mouth. For some reason they were defending a person who had staged a coup, a person who in the final analysis had also put a lawful authority up in front of a firing squad, and who had failed to justify his actions in any way.

When I was in Lithuania during the notorious events of January 1991, I recalled an interview I'd heard with two deputies. The correspondent asked them to give their assessment of what was happening in Lithuania. One of them began to yell, foaming at the mouth, that he was categorically opposed, that tomorrow they'd all gather on the Manezh Square to defend democracy, and so forth. The other said that without full and reliable information, he didn't consider himself entitled to express an opinion. In my view, this is the kind of approach that our wonderful mass media were lacking in then, and unfortunately, a lot of them are lacking in it to this day.

You mentioned something about a young woman who was carrying away the wounded at Ostankino....

I wasn't at Ostankino myself, but this woman was with us at the White House as well. I don't know her last name, but we called her Nika. She was seventeen years old. At Ostankino she dragged away six wounded, crawling in under the bullets and hauling them out. There was one case I know of: when a burst from a heavy-caliber machine gun tore a hand off one of the wounded, she tied a tourniquet on his arm to stop the bleeding. At that moment, an explosive shell hit him in the head, and literally splattered his brains over a wall. Ten minutes later, in shock, the woman again crawled out to drag away more wounded. She was at the White House, and did the same there....

A lot of people went to Ostankino, in trucks, on buses, on the metro or on foot. But only one truckload of people had weapons. As the demonstrators themselves relate, the troops opened fire on them suddenly. They were shooting not only from the main building of the Ostankino television center, but also from the building opposite.

Rumors have been spread persistently, saying that everything inside Ostankino has been shot up, and that rooms full of equipment have been put out of service. This last Sunday [October 31], I was at Ostankino taking part in a production. I saw individual bullet holes in the glass on the first floor, but I didn't see the total destruction that occurred at the White House. Inside, I didn't find any trace of the fighting at all. I purposely walked along the corridors, and I didn't see any walls riddled with bullets or anything of the sort.

(Tape recording)

Lyudmila Surova
I SAW THIS, AND DID NOT GO OUT OF MY MIND....
Report from the scene of the shooting

Two hours have passed since we escaped from beneath the gunfire, and we simply have to relate what we saw and heard. We don't have the right to remain silent in front of the people who helped us save our lives.

....We know perfectly well what an organized crowd is like, whether it is military or civilian, and we are not likely to confuse the spirit of an organized social action with the free expression of people's wills. Here we saw people who were not at all organized. They came in response to their own impulses, but those were impulses of protest. Against what? To the extent that we were able to grasp their fragmentary remarks, it was protest against the fraudulent democracy which has been transformed so abruptly into total dictatorship. Why did people go to the television center? Because it has been a long time since the mass media have seen such a denial of glasnost as has been witnessed in the past year. Once, a spell was cast on Russia using the words "exploitation" and "exploiter," but now we are lulled to sleep by the word "democracy."

....Of course, people are all different. Some are more gentle, or more intelligent. Others are more belligerent, as we later came to appreciate. But the people did not come in order to kill, or to avenge themselves; this was not an act of vengeance. They came to declare themselves. What did we see in the way of weapons? Five or six metal shields; one cudgel; someone had a piece of water pipe; and one young man of about fifteen had a hatchet, the type yardkeepers use to chop at the ice.... There were flags—anarchist flags, red flags, and white, yellow, and black tricolors. But most of the people who went past us went either empty-handed, or with the usual shopping bags and handbags. We did not see any detachments of armed fighters. This sparse procession did not suggest the possibility of armed actions, so we decided to go to the television center as well, to see for ourselves what happened there. As the phrase goes, to be eyewitnesses to events. If we had known what events!

"Makashov is speaking at the television center," a woman standing on the side of the road told us. As we drew closer, we began listening to what was being said—vulgar abuse, amplified by a megaphone: "Come out, you rats! Rats! Everyone who comes out voluntarily will get to keep one...ball! Come out, rats! There's no point resisting, Yeltsin has betrayed you. You're surrounded by the overwhelming forces of the enemy."

In front of the main television center people were standing on a truck, and it was from there that these words were coming.

....The doors of both buildings were closed and barred. A few men climbed onto the flat roof of a concrete structure, evidently part of the ventilation system. This wasn't high, about two meters, and was next to the edge of the pedestrian underpass. It was very easy to climb up. It was this that was soon to save our lives. Things livened up. A shout of triumph, "Hoora-a-h!" rang out along the road. We stuck our necks out, and walked in the direction of this "Hoorah!" "Mama, can I climb on the roof?" My son headed off from me some five or six meters toward the edge of the underpass.... And suddenly—Bang! A huge flash, flames up to the second floor, and at the same time as the "Hoorah!" which had not yet died away, furious gunfire from the second and third floors of the television center.

People literally dropped to the ground. Everyone threw themselves down instantly behind the God-given concrete wall. Here there was a truck of some kind. Between this truck and the wall of the ventilation structure there must have been fifty people. The firing did not stop for some five or seven minutes. Everyone was deeply shaken. We huddled together and craned our necks, since we still didn't know just where the shooting was coming from. In front of us was the building of the Russian television center, and only a truck was protecting us from it. If they started shooting out of it, we would all be killed....

....The fire slackened. No, it didn't stop, but the shots became more sparse and chaotic.

...."People have been wounded! We have to take the wounded away!" A huge heavy man with a broad face and clenched teeth was dragged from the side of the road and laid at my feet. "Where's he wounded?" "In the stomach." Several men went off, or more precisely, ran off, in order to bring back other victims. There seemed to be a lot of wounded. I tried to rub the sweat from the brow of the man I was attending to, and to my astonishment, started singing.... I sang loudly for some reason, though my ear for music is nothing special and I have no voice. Perhaps I thought my son would respond. There he was! Behind the wall! Alive! He couldn't run over to me—the space between us was being raked constantly with gunfire. It's true, people were running across, but I was scared to call him in case he didn't make it. *They're shooting at people in full flight! They're shooting at people who are dragging away the wounded!...* The bullets were whistling and cracking, some crisply, others with a resounding thud. "That's from a heavy-caliber machine gun," someone knowledgeable explained.

....After forty-five minutes of one-sided shooting, people suddenly started firing from the building nearest to us. From this, we had no cover whatsoever. A quite different sound overwhelmed us; the sky began to whine above our heads. We tried simply to press ourselves to the earth. The gunfire flew over our heads, quite literally in long white streaks.... Some defenders appeared; three brave people diverted the fire of the hardened marksmen in the television center. Some of the people who were taking cover with us decided to make a run for it. The distance to the nearest buildings was two hundred meters, but the danger zone that was under constant fire was less, seventy or a hundred meters. How could this distance be covered? Beneath the bullets it was terrifying. It was also strange and incomprehensible—why had they suddenly opened fire on us? We were all unarmed. It's true—none of the people taking cover with us had any weapons. I was told that a man in camouflage dress with a shaved head and a Kalashnikov rifle had run off, and that was all....

Two ambulances appeared further back along the road. They didn't drive up to us, though we shouted to them. But someone drove up a water truck with an orange tank. "Hang on, Dmitriy Pavlovich, now it's going to hurt." The men laid one of the wounded on a shield and pushed him into the cabin. The driver was standing almost upright. They were shooting! Why were they shooting at him? Where? Who was shooting at the wounded?...

(*Nezavisimaya Gazeta,* October 16, 1993)

Irina Mastykina
THEY DIED WITHOUT WEAPONS IN THEIR HANDS

....On October 3, Andrey Vuraki didn't take his girlfriend with him. After Gaidar's television speech, he went to Ostankino with his two best friends. At the instant when the beam of a searchlight in the television center lit up the crowd of people, the three were standing on the far side of the pond. "Everyone lie down, or we'll open fire!" came a shout from the searchlight. Everyone in the group obeyed. Then immediately, the troops opened fire on the defenseless people.

A burst of automatic fire stitched the three of them. A hollow-centered bullet pierced Andrey's spine, and tumbling end over end, turned his internal organs into a bloody mess. He was carried away by medical orderlies with whom he had once undergone practical training (Vuraki was a fifth-year student in the Medical Academy, and was studying to be a surgeon). They recognized him, but only on the following day were they able to inform his relatives of what had happened. The Vurakis had a new telephone number, and it took time to find out what it was. Andrey's parents were not to find their son alive; he died on the operating table.

One of his friends lived a little longer. He was buried yesterday in a different cemetery. The third friend was the lucky one. The same spinning bullet struck him in the arm. He is now in the Sklifosovskiy Institute, and was unable to attend the funerals.

Many other people did attend, even ones who had never seen Andrey Vuraki alive. A thick carpet of flowers covered the fresh mound of the grave on the very edge of the Babushkinskaya Cemetery. At the head of the grave stood a canopy of wreaths. There was also a photograph which his mother could barely tear away from her breast. It showed a handsome, broadly smiling young man. He was only twenty-one years old.

(*Komsomolskaya Pravda,* October 8, 1993)

Valeriy Vyzhutovich
THE DECISION TO HALT BROADCASTING ON THE
OSTANKINO CHANNEL ON THE EVENING OF OCTOBER 3
WAS MADE BY CHERNOMYRDIN
(Interview with Vyacheslav Bragin, head of the Ostankino Television and Radio Company)

....I wouldn't want to jump to conclusions, but there's a great deal that's strange, suspicious, and perhaps even treacherous about the way they defended Ostankino ... I called around all the phone numbers, trying to get through to Yerin, Golushko, and Grachev, but their aides fobbed me off onto their deputies. In the end I could only get through to Yerin. He told me: "Don't panic, I've got the situation under control, reinforcements will arive soon."

Who else in the government did you talk to that night?

I talked to Chernomyrdin fifteen or twenty times, and to Shumeiko just as often. I also talked to Filatov, Krasavchenko, and Poltoranin .... I phoned around all the members of the government, and all they said was, "Hold on, hold on...." You see, all of them, as if by agreement, were giving only verbal help.

And this strikes you as strange, suspicious, and treacherous?

Not just this. Eyewitnesses have told me that the militia gave the green light to trucks and buses that were going to Ostankino. I was naive enough to phone the Interior Ministry and say, "Stop them, block the road, you've got the traffic police!" ....Meanwhile, there's a militia headquarters not far from Ostankino. The chief there, whose name I'd rather not give, told me later that on the evening of October 3 he received an order to withdraw his unit further from the television center. Doesn't this seem strange? Doesn't it seem strange that the Tulskaya division of the Interior Ministry forces, whose help had been promised us, never arrived? I had the distinct feeling that everyone had abandoned us. I don't think this was by chance. Someone, it seems, wanted to get even with Ostankino. I'm not thinking only of Anpilov and Makashov here.

Who else, then?

I'm afraid to speculate on this topic. Let's just say that some third force was interested in seeing the television center stormed.

Doesn't it seem to you that someone was very reluctant to see the armed actions at the television center recorded on videotape, and especially, to see a general picture of the fighting recorded?

I find it hard to suspect anyone. But I would like to firmly deny any suspicions people might have of me. There have already been conjectures that, let's say, I was waiting to see who would finish on top. Nothing of the sort. That night I gave interviews to Radio Freedom and Moscow Echo in which I clearly and explicitly declared my attitude to the insurgents, calling them criminals and bandits.

You would have expressed this attitude more convincingly, and most important, professionally, if you'd ensured that the journalists of Ostankino were able to get on the air. But as many camera operators and television journalists have said, you stopped them from being given cameras. Why?

Because their lives are more valuable to me than any television coverage. I don't have the right to send people out under bullets.

These people are journalists. To be on the scene of events—and yes, sometimes under bullets, however painful this might be—is their professional duty.

And my duty, the duty of the director, is to save them from getting killed. This is what I tried to do on that terrible night.

(*Izvestiya,* October 13, 1993)

Aleksey Tsvetkov
FREEDOM ON THE BARRICADES

....An attractive, brown-eyed young woman persuaded us to get into a truck and to go to the television center.... After they bluntly refused to let us on the air, it became obvious that we weren't going to achieve anything with speeches. The people burst through the fence and ran up to the walls. A grenade launcher was fired somewhere, and answering fire opened up. I received a powerful blow in the face from a shield, and all the events grew hazy and became mixed together.

A ZiL truck poked its snout into the glass wall, and without paying any heed to the shooting, people rushed into the building. The darkness was full of explosions and bullets, and clouds of choking gas rolled out of it. A now-familiar young man in a worn leather coat fired ahead of himself and, pulling on a gas mask, dived into the opening. Disorderly shooting was going on from everywhere, and some buses were blocking the road. Then an armored personnel carrier appeared, apparently one of those which mysteriously vanished from the square at the Supreme Soviet before the cordon was breached. Everyone froze. Time stopped still. We waited. The APC turned its machine gun and fired a long burst into the television center. Glass flew everywhere. But before people had a chance to shout "Hoorah!" the APC again turned its turret, and began firing on the crowd.

I lay beneath a lime tree not far from the pond. To move now was extremely difficult. Heavy fire was being directed at anything that moved—the machine gun in the revolving turret of the APC didn't fall silent even for a minute. They fired even at the treetops, obviously thinking that attackers were sitting in the branches. After ten minutes, I was covered with leaves and twigs, like a hedgehog preparing for winter. An old man with his head covered with blood fell down next to me. He was in shock,

and couldn't understand a thing. I dragged him to the road, also with little idea of whether I was doing the right thing....
(*Obshchaya Gazeta*, September 29–October 4, 1993)

Nataliya Gevorkyan and Aleksandr Zhilin
THE PRESIDENT'S TRAP, AND A TRAP FOR THE PRESIDENT
Extract from the speech by Defense Minister Pavel Grachev at a press conference on October 6:

"According to reports by the Interior Ministry, [at Ostankino] there were about four thousand unarmed and about one hundred armed people. Confronting them were four hundred Interior Ministry and special forces troops, and six armored personnel carriers. When the armed actions began, a further fifteen APCs and a hundred militia personnel were sent there. Within ten minutes of the guard opening fire, the crowd had fled from the scene. It has been said that this was in order to prepare for a second assault. But this is untrue; there was no drastic danger present."
(*Moskovskie Novosti*, October 17, 1993)

Vladimir Lopatin: Five Questions from a Soldier

The first question: Why, when the attempt to storm Ostankino began at 8.15 p.m., were the personnel and equipment needed to defend the television center not there, even though Rutskoi had called at 4 p.m. for the assault to take place?

The second question: Why did Gaidar appeal to the people to come to the Moscow Soviet, to Staraya Square and to the Vasilievskiy Embankment at 10 p.m., even though a presidential decree issued at 4 p.m. had imposed a state of emergency, banning meetings and demonstrations? Were these provisions of the decree enacted?

The third question: Why did the OMON forces and the Interior Ministry troops quickly retreat before the defenders of the White House at the mayor's office? And why were flamethrowers abandoned at the mayor's office, as though on purpose?

The fourth question: Why did the minister of defense implement the order to send troops to the positions specified only at 9:30 in the morning, although he received this order at 3 a.m.?
(*Obshchaya Gazeta*, October 8–14, 1993)

A wounded defender of the White House is carried out by the OMON. The government forces quickly occupied the first two floors of the White House on October 4, and by midafternoon the fighting had become sluggish as they moved on the central tower.

[Photo by Vojtech Lavicka]

ASSAULT ON THE HOUSE OF SOVIETS

During the night of October 3-4, Yeltsin received the Defense Ministry's agreement to use the regular army against the opposition. When it became clear that the Ostankino television center was not in danger, Vice President Yegor Gaidar appealed to Yeltsin's supporters by radio to go in to the center of the city to defend the institutions of the government. By midnight, about ten thousand people were concentrated on Tverskaya Street, from the Kremlin to Pushkin Square. They began to construct barricades.

Yeltsin signed a decree to dissolve the Moscow Soviet and local soviets in Moscow. The militia and OMON occupied soviet buildings and arrested dozens of deputies, beating some of them brutally. Around 3 a.m. on October 4, Yeltsin signed a written order for the Defense Ministry. Pro-Yeltsin detachments and groups, selected from divisions located around

Moscow, began to move toward the center of the city. Around the same time, a few small armed groups of officers and soldiers who supported the opposition were stopped outside Moscow.

Inside the House of Soviets, the opposition made no further defense plans. There were stocks of arms and ammunition inside the House of Soviets, but opposition leaders and military commanders refused to distribute them among volunteers.

At 6:45 a.m. on October 4, armored personnel carriers began to attack the barricades the opposition had put up around the House of Soviets. About a thousand unarmed people were standing in front of the House of Soviets to defend it. In Free Russia Square in front of the House of Soviets, pro-Yeltsin forces opened fire on the crowd from machine guns and heavy machine guns. Dozens were killed and wounded.

Over the course of the next hour, pro-Yeltsin troops shot at the building and then began to storm it. From buildings around the House of Soviets, snipers shot at any sign of motion inside or outside the building.

The offensive side rapidly occupied two floors of the six-story section of the House of Soviets, slowly pushing the defenders upstairs. But in the central tower of the building, all attacks were repelled. After midday, the fight inside the building became sluggish, but the shooting on the building from outside, from all types of arms, was continuous. Between 10 and 11 a.m., four tanks opened cannon fire on the House of Soviets. The building caught fire.

Around midday, talks began between the defenders and the commanders of the attacking forces. By 4 p.m., Rutskoi had agreed to put down arms and surrender to save the lives of about two thousand unarmed people—people's deputies of Russia, Supreme Soviet staff, journalists, political activists, and rank-and-file supporters of the Supreme Soviet.

After the surrender, many supporters of the opposition were beaten and even shot by the militia and OMON in neighboring streets and courtyards after leaving the House of Soviets. The hunt continued all through the night of October 4–5. Twenty-nine people were killed and 107 were wounded by firearms after the surrender.

The Night Before the Attack

During the night, troops began to be brought into Moscow. This was the first time the Ministry of Defense had become involved in the conflict. In no case was the whole of a large unit brought into the operation. A careful selection was made of individual subunits whose loyalty could be relied upon. The following troops were assembled for the attack: a single brigade of Interior Ministry forces, quartered in Moscow in the Teply Stan district and previously subject to the KGB of the USSR; several subunits of the Tamanskaya and Kantemirovskaya mechanized divisions, which brought with them ten tanks with specially selected crews made up of officers; subunits of the Tulskaya airborne division that were quartered near Naro-Fominsk; a subunit of the OMON, and several dozen volunteers from an organization of Afghan war veterans (veterans of the Afghan war were also among the defenders of the House of Soviets). The Dzerzhinskiy division of Interior Ministry forces, which was regarded as less reliable after a number of soldiers had gone over to the side of the Supreme Soviet, was used to seal off the territory around the House of Soviets. Konstantin Kobets, Deputy Minister of Defense, headed the special staff that was formed that night to command the assembled forces.

During the evening of October 3, Russian Vice-Premier Yegor Gaidar appeared on television and appealed to Moscow residents to come out onto the streets next to the Kremlin and the Moscow Soviet building, in order to defend the institutions of the government against attacks by supporters of the Supreme Soviet. This appeal was in open violation of the state of emergency decree, which had banned all meetings and demonstrations. Not for the first time, however, the Russian authorities ignored one of their own decrees.

The supporters of the Supreme Soviet simply did not have the strength to seize government buildings. For the sake of justice it should be said that the building of the press agency RIA-TASS at the Nikitskie Gates was taken over for a short time, but it was then abandoned without a fight. The mass media reported an attempt to capture the building of the General Staff, but in fact there was no more than a picket by a few dozen unarmed people, who appealed unsuccessfully to the guards to go over to the side of the Supreme Soviet.

Meanwhile, a crowd of thousands of people gathered at the Moscow Soviet. It was already known that the opposition had not succeeded in occupying the television center, and a report had already been circulated that forces loyal to the president were being brought into Moscow. No hostile acts by supporters of the Supreme Soviet were observed in the vicinity of government buildings. Nevertheless, supporters of Yeltsin began erecting barricades—rather substantial ones—on which they spent the whole night and all the following day. Even when the House of Soviets was being pounded by tank cannons, and after almost all its defenders had surrendered, many supporters of the president continued defending these barricades—it is not clear against whom.

As we ourselves noted, the crowd that came into the streets in response to Gaidar's summons was quite diverse. One could observe members of the intelligentsia, a number of ecstatic pensioners, more than a few curious onlookers (confining their curiosity to areas of the city where no shooting was going on), and a good many of the people normally to be found hanging around commercial kiosks.

While the public were gathering on the street near the Moscow Soviet, the building itself was occupied by the OMON. The deputies who were there were arrested, despite their legal immunity from arrest (this had not been abolished under Decree No. 1400, which ended the powers only of the people's deputies of Russia, and guaranteed the rights of the local organs of representative power). Only a few deputies succeeded in avoiding arrest, fleeing the complex of Moscow Soviet buildings before the OMON blockade was complete. These deputies managed to take with them cassette tapes containing recordings of radio communications between personnel of the Interior Ministry throughout the whole period of the conflict.

Also arrested were deputies of the Moscow Soviet who had gone to the offices of various regional soviets, and deputies of these regional soviets themselves. The buildings of the regional soviets were seized. Outside the building of the Oktyabrskaya regional soviet late in the evening of October 3, three of our friends and fellow members of the Party of Labor were arrested; these were the Moscow Soviet deputies Boris Kagarlitsky and Vladimir Kondratov, and Federation of Independent Trade Unions of Russia press secretary Aleksandr Segal. A number of other people were arrested at the same time. In several militia stations where they were taken, the detainees were subjected to frequent beatings. The militia demanded that they confess to absurd charges of having hijacked a militia vehicle and led an armed group which killed two militia members. Numerous other detainees were also beaten, some of them without the slightest cause.

Inside the House of Soviets the prevailing mood, which had risen somewhat with the breaking of the blockade and the storming of the mayor's office, began to fall. Reports began arriving of the slaughter at Ostankino, and the first wounded began to be brought in. Hopes that the morale of the troops was about to crack, and that they would support the Supreme Soviet, were not being borne out. Although there were attempts by groups of military personnel to act in support of the Supreme Soviet, these were crushed, and detachments which tried to reach Moscow were arrested. On October 3 the commander of a brigade of Interior Ministry forces from Sofrino refused to open fire on the defenders of the Supreme Soviet, preferring to remain true to his oath. On orders from the commander, the brigade left its position at the mayor's office, but only a few of its troops crossed over to the side of the defenders of the House of Soviets.

As radio communications were intercepted indicating that troops loyal to the president were moving on the center of Moscow, it became clear that an assault was being prepared. However, no additional measures were taken to defend the House of Soviets. The promises to hand out weapons to volunteers remained only promises, but gave rise to a mass of rumors to the effect that automatic rifles were being handed out in the White House to anyone who asked for them, in whatever quantities they wanted.

Although government propagandists stated that the commanders of the pro-Yeltsin forces did their best to keep bloodshed to a minimum, steps were taken that indicated the exact opposite. Throughout the evening and all through the night, the press center of the Chief Administration of Internal Affairs of Moscow used the militia radio stations to broadcast information about the two militia members who had been killed in the clashes on October 3. The heads of the Interior Ministry were under no illusions as to the moods such information would arouse in the militia, the OMON, and the Interior Ministry troops. "We'll slaughter all of them!" "No prisoners!"— such were the sentiments pouring out continually over the airwaves.

No warning was given of the attack, and no offer was made to allow unarmed people to leave the Supreme Soviet building. Attempts by the leadership of the Supreme Soviet and by individual deputies to appeal to the government for talks on the fate of the unarmed people in the House of Soviets were rejected; the government simply had no wish to listen.

In the morning many supporters of the Supreme Soviet had left the White House. Reasoning that an assault was possible only at night, that it would not take place during the morning or afternoon, they set off home in order to rest. Others considered defending the White House impossible from a military point of view, and did not wish to die in vain. Still others were ready to defend the constitutional order, but were unwilling to perish in order to save such political figures as Rutskoi and Khasbulatov. However, thousands of people around the House of Soviets and inside it decided to stay and to defend their last stronghold.

TESTIMONY OF TWO EYEWITNESSES

(Recorded by Nadezhda Bondarenko, who says: "This was told to me by two people, a woman and a man. They are remote from politics and quite disinclined to violence. I have tried to avoid changing anything in their account, even things with which I cannot agree...."

....On the evening of October 3, I went with a companion to look for a missing relative. We knew that he might be on the barricades around the White House. We simply wanted to try to persuade him to go home. Around the White House there were militia members, or troops of the OMON, or Interior Ministry troops—I don't know exactly.... But they let us through freely, although they searched the men. Next to the White House, people were building barricades. There were all sorts of people there, and in all sorts of moods. My companion suddenly started helping them drag some pipes for building barricades, though at first he hadn't been going to do that. On the other hand, there were also people there who were gripped by a single thought, a single idea, and for precisely this reason, I consider, they couldn't think objectively.... I personally saw Cossacks, religious believers, and simple young people who didn't have any clearly defined views.... They were united by hatred for Yeltsinism, for the situation that had arisen in the country. In the White House itself people understood more clearly what they wanted, and their actions struck me as more purposeful. But personally I've never been involved in politics, and in general I just wanted everything to be over as quickly as possible....

Then my companion and I lost one another in the crowd. What happened to him after that, he can tell you himself.

Testimony of Boris Kagarlitsky

On Sunday morning I wasn't in Moscow. I'd gone for the day to visit my family outside the city, and I only managed to return toward eight in the evening. By this time there was already shooting around Ostankino, the first and fourth television channels were off the air, and the second channel was broadcasting a test pattern. When I went to the building of the Krasnopresnenskiy Regional Soviet, there was hardly anyone there either. The OMON had gone over to the side of the parliament, and had been sent off somewhere else. With the breaking of the blockade, the deputies of the Russian Federation had flocked into the White House.

On the door of the chairperson of the regional soviet, Aleksandr Krasnov, was a decree of President Rutskoi under which Krasnov was named as mayor of Moscow. This was the cherished dream of the chairperson of the Krasnopresnenskiy Soviet. When Popov resigned in 1992, Krasnov put forward his candidacy for the post of mayor and even conducted an election campaign, although it was clear to everyone that there wouldn't be any elections. Expensive, colorful posters with the portrait of Krasnov, the "candidate of the Party of Muscovites," were pasted up around the city. Some incalculable sum was spent, but to no result—Yeltsin simply appointed Luzhkov to take Popov's place. Now, without any elections, Krasnov could feel himself to be the ruler of the city—at least for a few hours.

After congratulating Krasnov on his appointment, I asked him which particular city services were under his control. It became clear that the new administrator of the Russian capital himself had no idea. "You try and work it out," he urged. Sadly, there was nothing left except to follow his advice. By this time Vladimir Kondratov and Aleksandr Segal, the Press Secretary of the Federation of Independent Trade Unions of Russia, had arrived. We set off together to the White House, hoping that there, at least, we could obtain some information.

On this night the center of Moscow presented a strange spectacle. A multitude of unarmed people were swarming around the parliament building, discussing the latest news. Then unexpectedly, commandeered trucks appeared from somewhere, full of agitated people demanding weapons. They reported that there had been dozens of dead and wounded at Ostankino, and were asking for help. Receiving neither weapons nor assistance, they once again set off somewhere. Within the

White House itself, an unbelievable chaos reigned. As before, there were no lights. During the afternoon, after the lifting of the blockade, the lights had been turned on for a time, but not for long. The elevators were not working, and we had to climb the stairs.

In a corridor on one of the upper floors we came upon General Albert Makashov, whom the pro-Yeltsin press later named as one of the main instigators of the "carefully planned and prepared revolt." The general was running along the corridor, fastening up a bulletproof vest as he went, and was shouting: "I've no weapons! I've no people! There won't be any help! Go and install soviet power yourselves!"

To be fair, it should be pointed out that in the Kremlin that same evening Sergey Parkhomenko, a journalist for the newspaper *Segodnya*, witnessed a similar spectacle. Among the members of the government, panic reigned; Yeltsin had completely lost control of the situation, and was merely questioning those about him in order to find out what was going on. In Parkhomenko's words, the scene was reminiscent of a madhouse.

Some time later, however, the "gray cardinals" of the regime, Gennadiy Burbulis and Mikhail Poltoranin, appeared in the Kremlin. They effectively assumed command, and quickly enforced order among the distracted members of the government. These two knew perfectly well that there was no serious threat. To judge from everything, it was they who had devised the scenario of a decisive battle—the very scenario that was now being put into effect.

The possibility is not excluded that the authors of the scenario were provoking not only Rutskoi and Khasbulatov, but also their own chief. But this is not important. One way or another, the situation was under control. Rutskoi did not have any serious forces, and the people who had obeyed his summons and gone to Ostankino had fallen into a carefully prepared trap. Burbulis and Poltoranin had triumphed. All that now remained to them was to put down the revolt and to settle accounts with their adversaries, teaching a lesson to anyone who might dare to speak out against the regime for a long time to come.

While we were still in the Krasnopresnenskiy Regional Soviet, we had learned that Luzhkov's forces were blockading the Moscow Soviet. The members of the anti-crisis staff were locked in their offices. Meanwhile, Vice-Premier Yegor Gaidar had used the second television channel, the only one that was working, to summon supporters of the regime to gather outside the Moscow Soviet building. These "volunteers," it was apparent, were to help the OMON capture the building. They behaved in an extremely aggressive, even boorish manner.

Meanwhile, after failing to obtain coherent information about what was happening in the city, Segal, Kondratov, and I found a ride with a car that was going to the Oktyabrskaya Regional Council. There we met with Dmitriy Krymov and other regional deputies, whom we knew well as a result of their opposition to corrupt property deals around Gagarin Square. The conversations we had in the regional soviet building did not increase our optimism. Troops were being brought to the center of the city, while the supporters of the parliament were mostly unarmed, and without real leadership.

While we were sitting with our colleagues from the regional soviet, armored personnel carriers were passing along Leninskiy Prospekt. The chairperson of the soviet tried for some reason to discover whether the machines bore the insignia of guard units. If there were, this meant the vehicles belonged to the Tamanskaya division. If not, that meant they belonged to the Interior Ministry forces. As if that now had the slightest significance....

Leaving the building of the soviet, we stopped next to the vehicle that had brought us from the White House. This vehicle was a four-wheel-drive UAZ belonging to the militia. Both the supporters of the parliament and the Yeltsinites had many of these vehicles, since both the White House guard and Luzhkov's OMON were considered subunits of the militia. A number of other activists who had also come from the White House were standing with us near the vehicle. Some of them proposed that we return to the parliament, others suggested that we visit other regional soviets, and still others thought we should disperse and head home.

While we were holding this discussion, a car stopped next to us. Four people in civilian clothing and carrying automatic rifles leapt out of it. Over their jackets they were wearing bulletproof vests. Two of them smelt strongly of liquor. After the lads in the bulletproof vests, a man in the uniform of a militia colonel (minus the cap) and with a large old-style automatic rifle climbed from the car. Astonishingly, he really was a militia officer. After cocking his rifle, he ordered us to raise our hands and stand in line.

Threatening to blow our brains out if we so much as moved, the guardians of law and order searched us, and then, in two vehicles which had driven up, took us to Militia Station No. 2 in the Polyanka neighborhood. Here they stood us with our faces to the wall, and after hitting us around the legs and on our backs a few times as a warning, took us off to be interrogated separately. They questioned us on how we came to be next to a militia vehicle, on where we had been before we came to the regional soviet, and on our political views.

Our deputies' cards did not arouse any respect in them—rather the reverse. While one militia member was questioning me in very proper fashion, another ran into the room from time to time and slammed his fist into my back or head. Then he again ran off somewhere about his business, but on the way back, again burst in on us and hit me once more. This was accompanied by shouts such as, "You wanted democracy, you sons of bitches? We'll show you democracy!" I was surprised to find that among themselves, the militia members used thieves' jargon, and did not refer to one another except as "dicks" and "pigs." In the militia station next day, we met a racketeer who had been arrested. This man, by contrast, spoke Russian in a perfectly correct manner.

After questioning us and beating us some more, the guardians of law and order from Militia Station No. 2 admitted that they had nothing on us. But they could not yet let us go, since a curfew was in force in the city, and it was already midnight. They promised to release us in the morning. They took our valuables, notebooks, and deputies' cards from us, saying that they would return them in the morning. We were taken off to the cells.

Next morning, instead of setting us free as promised, they loaded us into a militia UAZ with our hands bound behind our backs, and took us off to Militia Station No. 77. Here they informed me that under a Yeltsin decree the Moscow Soviet had been disbanded, the immunity of deputies had been revoked, and that we were charged with ... stealing a militia vehicle. The UAZ in which we had travelled from the White House had, it was later explained, been abandoned by the militia near Ostankino. It had then been used to transport wounded, and had made several trips to one place and another, with the drivers constantly changing.

Leonid Ilyushenko, the last behind the wheel, had been given the vehicle at the White House by one of the commanders of the spontaneously-formed volunteer corps. He could not say precisely where the vehicle had come from either, but after he had been interrogated under torture, the militia explained everything to him. Almost unconscious from the blows, he signed a number of statements according to which he was supposed to have stolen the vehicle at the instigation of Moscow Soviet Deputies Kondratov and Kagarlitsky. These maleficent deputies, showing him their identity cards, had forced him to hijack the militia UAZ. Along with gun-toting companions, they had then driven around the city, issuing orders to armed insurgents.

At the same time as the investigators' evidence had us driving around the capital, more than a dozen people had seen us in totally different places. I had mostly been at the dacha, while Kondratov was working in the Krasnopresnenskiy Regional Soviet many kilometers from Ostankino. But no one was perturbed by this. In essence, the affair was not about us at all. Compromising evidence was needed against the Moscow Soviet, in order to explain to the public why it had been necessary to disband the soviet and deprive the deputies of their immunity. As in the Terekhov affair, all that remained was to obtain open-hearted confessions from us.

They acted simply and according to habit. Kondratov and Segal were handcuffed, and beaten with clubs on the back and legs. Then Kondratov had his head beaten against a bulletproof vest. I was not spared; they hit my head against a grating and against a wall, and then beat me on the shoulders with a rifle butt. After the second blow I almost fell to the floor. This could have ended very badly, had not one of the militia members literally torn me from the hands of his colleagues. Another militia member in an army bulletproof vest dragged me from the room where the beatings were going on and pushed me into a cell with the others.

However severely they beat the deputies, they beat the other prisoners even more ferociously. This was in an effort to milk them of new statements against us, and simply as a warning. All the people who had been passengers in the UAZ were being held in one place. Also dragged in here were other people who had been arrested in different places, in some cases totally at random. Unwilling to investigate each separate case, they listed all the detainees as "passengers in a militia vehicle." Soon the number of "passengers" on the list reached fourteen. That vehicle seemed destined for a place in the Guinness Book of Records.

We sat behind the bars. Shouts and the sound of blows, accompanied by swearing, carried through to us from the corridor. This alternated with reports on the militia radio, which spoke of hundreds of dead in the city, and of the storming of the White House. One of the militia officers brought two grenades into the militia station, and every militia officer who came in tried without fail to discover how these were supposed to work. The militia called in the army engineers, but the engineers were delayed; meanwhile, the weary and occasionally half-drunk minions of the law several times came close to blowing up themselves and us together.

So long as no one knew where we were being held, the militia could do whatever they wanted with us. But toward evening we managed to get out a message to the effect that we were in Militia Station No. 77. My wife contacted several friends and the leadership of the trade unions. Within a few minutes all the details of our fate were in the international computer networks. After another half hour telephone calls started pouring into the militia station from Tokyo, London, and New York, from foreign newspapers and human rights organizations. Some time later, a phone call came from the presidential administration, demanding that the scandal be quelled immediately. Presidential Council member Sergey Karaganov, arriving in a luxurious BMW, explained to the militia chief that it was imperative that the deputies be released. This independent initiative later cost Karaganov serious unpleasantness; he had not been appointed to the Presidential Council in order to defend the rights of oppositionists.

Soon the militia member on duty took to answering the incessant calls by repeating distractedly, "They've already been released." "It's not true!" we shouted from behind the bars. Eventually, we were freed along with all the prisoners except the driver of the UAZ, out of whom the militia now began beating new affidavits.

Late on the night of October 4, we made it home. By this time, the White House had already fallen, and a new order reigned in the city. The building of the Moscow Soviet had been seized late in the evening of October 3, roughly an hour after we had been arrested. The guards submitted to the orders from the mayor, and behaved in proper fashion. The "volunteers," on the other hand, showed their true colors. Several offices were sacked and looted. One of the guards who tried to stop the excesses of the "democratic activists" was beaten up.

All the members of the anti-crisis team were arrested, after remaining at their posts until the last minute. Among those arrested was the human rights defender Viktor Bulgakov, imprisoned for the first time while Stalin was still alive. Others detained included Lena Klimenko and Yura Khramov, who had been promised awards for their previous defense of the White House; the former dissident Viktor Kuzin; and the former KGB officer Aleksandr Tsopov. Deputy Chairperson of the Moscow Soviet Yuriy Sedykh-Bondarenko was one of the last to leave the building; after first being blockaded in his office, he was removed and, after interrogation, sent to prison. Aleksandr Popov was luckier. The guards got him out of the cordoned-off building. He issued the last report of the Press Center of the Moscow Soviet from a pay telephone on the street.

The premises and equipment of the press center were promptly handed over to the press service of the mayor's office. Here, a real pogrom was staged. Not only were papers pulled from the shelves and everything turned upside down, but for some reason a fax machine was burned out.

(Boris Kagarlitsky. Excerpts from the manuscript of *The Square Wheels*)

Interview with Aleksandr Strakhov (obtained by Andrei Kolganov)
Can you describe the events you witnessed on October 3 and 4?
Right at the beginning, I want to stress that I'm not relaying the impressions of anyone else. I'm going to talk only about what I witnessed myself, what I saw with my own eyes.

....On the evening of October 3, a report was broadcast saying that a state of emergency had been imposed in Moscow, and that meetings and demonstrations had been banned. Then, fifteen minutes later, I saw Vice-Premier Yegor Gaidar on the screen, calling on people to gather at the building of the Moscow Soviet to defend something and someone—it wasn't clear what. A few hours later, I received a message from the corps of deputies of the Moscow Soviet, saying that the chairperson of the Moscow Soviet, the deputy chairperson, and many of the deputies had been blockaded—or in effect, arrested—in one of the sections of the soviet building. In another section of the building, staff members were continuing to work, transmitting information about events until the people there were arrested as well.

I left home about 1 a.m. on the night of October 4, and made for the center of the city. Above all else, I considered it my duty to go to Red

Square. Between the Shrine of the Blessed Vasiliy and the Spasskaya Tower of the Kremlin, several hundred people had gathered. There was also a vehicle with loudspeakers, over which some television or radio broadcasts or other were being relayed, and one or two fires were burning. I was struck by the sight of Red Square absolutely dark—the first time I had ever seen it like that. It was lit up only by these fires. Between the Historical Museum and the Kremlin wall, a barricade had been constructed out of pipes and metal railings. A few fires were burning, and people were warming themselves.

I then walked along October 25 Street [Nikolskaya]. This was well lit. There were three barricades on the street, with as many as a hundred people on each. At the furthermost barricade, at Dzerzhinskiy Square, there were only fifteen or twenty people. Behind them was a line of bottles full of gasoline.

There was nothing particularly aggressive about the mood there—on the contrary, everything was very peaceful.

When I returned to Red Square and went past the Historical Museum to the Aleksandrovskiy Gardens, I heard the clicking of rifle-bolts. Looking around, I saw that on the Kremlin wall there were people in camouflage suits and in civilian clothing holding weapons. This was at about two o'clock in the morning.

What kind of uniform were these people in?

Camouflage gear. There were also people in civilian clothes. There I met a Catholic priest, with whom I made my way to the White House. From what I could tell he was interested, as I was, in discovering the mood of the people who had come out into the streets.

We went along Gorky Street. The first barricade we saw was immediately beyond the Central Telegraph Office, at the approach to the Moscow Artistic Theater. There were already a lot of people there.

How many?

I think about ten thousand. They were in the stretch between the Central Telegraph Office and Pushkin Square. I could be wrong, but I'd put the number at about that. There were three barricades—another barricade further along, and a third, final one on Pushkin Square. The largest concentration of people was on the square in front of the Moscow Soviet building. The gates leading into the laneway, to the entrances to the building, were shut. Behind the gates we could see armed people in uniform, a good many of them.

People were standing in groups, discussing what was happening. There were quite a few drunks, and also people I'd describe as ladies with lapdogs. I had the impression that, for the most part, the people there were just the casual public. Unquestionably, there were also people who had come in conscious response to Gaidar's appeal. They came there in order to do something, and there wouldn't have been any need to force them.

The feeling was much the same as during public festivities in earlier times—on holidays, Gorky Street was given over to the people. There was just this impression, with the only differences being that this was happening not during the daytime but at night, that there were barricades and agitated people, and that these people had come in response to a summons from an official figure.

The last barricade was on Pushkin Square at the House of the Actor. Then there was an armored personnel carrier, and beyond this a sort of no man's land. We turned into Tverskoy Boulevard, and headed towards Arbatskaya Square. Next to McDonald's, we saw a group of eighteen- or nineteen-year-olds who for no apparent reason began going up to the cars that were parked there and trying to break the windows. We asked, "Hey, what are you attacking the cars for?" To this, one of them replied, "We've seen everything here, so now we're going to have a look over there. And do you think we're going to go there on foot?" Then he went back to one of the cars. We made some further remarks, whereupon they pulled out two pistols and began firing in the air, saying, "Right, we've got a way of getting there." I can't say what kind of cartridges were in the pistols, but their determination to go and use the weapons in action was written all over their faces.

We walked along the boulevards, then along Kalininskiy Prospekt, and came to the mayor's office. The windows on the ground floor were broken. By this time, it was closer to four o'clock. We didn't hurry because we were trying to go up to every group of people, to work out what they were talking about, what they wanted, and how they viewed the situation. A little way off, closer to the bridge, some kind of structure had been erected. It would have been hard to call it a barricade, even by comparison with the barricades on Gorky Street. Behind this—well, let's call it a barricade—a couple of fires were burning, with people sitting and standing around them. We went up to the people, and listened to what they were saying. Here I'd note the following. Strange as it may seem, at these first two fires there were quite a few young people. I'd have put their age at about twenty-five. They were talking, and women were walking around with tea and something to eat (on Gorky Street there had also been an improvised buffet).

We turned right, and walked along next to the House of Soviets to the humpbacked bridge. Near the bridge, we crossed over a barricade. Here there were two or three barricades, but only a few people. There were more people further along, on a little square between the House of Soviets, the iron fence at the edge of a park, the bridge, and a small two-story building.

How many people were here?

Not so many. One and a half thousand, probably. There was no reason for a huge number of people to congregate there. They were scattered all over the square. Campfires were burning, and there were tents over to the right next to the iron fence.

And were there flags, signs, and so forth?

I didn't see any huge signs, though there were things written on the tents, slogans of all kinds. There were a lot of leaflets of every imaginable variety, proclamations, and newspaper clippings—including, I remember, two columns from the *Guardian*. They had been posted on the windows all along the ground floor of the House of Soviets. We tried diligently to read all of them.

On the lawn next to the two-story building was a wooden cross and twenty or thirty icons. Two priests in cassocks were standing there. People came up, prayed, and went away.

We probably spent two hours there, walking around. The square was relatively small. Someone then told me that the place was called Free Russia Square. The name sounds blasphemous, especially after what happened there later. At six o'clock the Catholic priest and I split up; I went back to the campfires to talk to people.

We had come to the White House to see who it was that the people in front of the Moscow Soviet had been mobilized against—who it was that they had been summoned to fight, who it was that had been described as red-browns [Communist-Fascists], bandits and rebels. In the

first place, it should be stated very clearly, we didn't see a single drunk there. Even though a great deal was said later about drunken bandits being at the White House, I stress—we didn't see a single drunk there.
And in front of the Moscow Soviet you did see them?
As I said earlier, at the Moscow Soviet quite a few people were in a less than sober condition. Festivities, public festivities—it was exactly that impression. On these occasions there always used to be a good number of tipsy people.

At the House of Soviets there was no sense of celebration, and perhaps as a result of this, there was a complete absence of drunks. There were people of all kinds, with all kinds of views. People said openly that they were not at all impressed by the existing parliament or by individual deputies. I can say the same for myself—I don't see all the deputies in a wonderful light, and I want to stress that what angers me above all is the way legality has been breached, to put it mildly. The important thing isn't the present make-up of the parliament, but the principle of respect for the law.

The people there had all sorts of opinions. There were anti-Semites, and their slogans could be seen around the place. But I want to stress that the people there had all sorts of views. They'd been brought together there by the violation of legality that took place on September 21. This was the common ground that united them. Plenty of the people present did not sympathize with communist teachings. People had gathered there beneath the banner of respect for the law, and not of Marxist-Leninist ideology or of progress toward reform. People of all ages were there, too. There were middle-aged people, and some who were old, obviously past seventy. Others were mere adolescents. As well as men, there were quite a few women, some of them no more than about fifteen years old.

I want to stress that no one was lounging around there, and no one was there for fun. There was a kind of thoughtful tension. This wasn't a celebration, in contrast to the scene on Gorky Street. Children were present, or, more precisely, parents with their children. People from various cities were there, as signs indicating where people had come from showed.

I continued walking around and talking to people, and began to express my own thoughts as well. For example, I find anti-Semitism repellent. At one of the campfires, I heard anti-Semitic views expressed loudly and categorically. I'm totally indifferent to the ethnicity of the people I talk to—whether they're Russian, Georgian, Jewish, black, or whatever. First and foremost, they're human beings, just as I am. I tried to explain this to the people I talked to around the campfires.

People there were discussing what had happened the day before at Ostankino and at the mayor's office, but I don't want to relate this, since I was neither at Ostankino nor at the mayor's office, and I don't consider myself qualified to discuss those events. But there is information about what happened there, and living people who were present. Let them tell their stories, just as I'm telling mine. No one there had any firearms. There were people with militia clubs, with pieces of pipe, and with sticks. Paving stones and rocks were piled up alongside the barricades. This was actually the case. But as for people armed with submachine guns or sniper rifles—there wasn't a single one.

(Tape recorded testimony)

Report by Oleg Vasilyev in the Echo-Conference SU.POL (fido.net), October 14, 1993

On the evening of October 3 I was also at the White House, and encountered a certain Kh..., who was going through the crowd next to the building and saying, "Anyone who wants a rifle, follow me." Naturally, I followed after him. He collected ten or fifteen people, lined them up, and recorded their last names. I asked him, "What, are you really going to give everyone a rifle?" He replied, "Yes."

N. N., member of a fighting detachment
TWELVE DAYS OF CRISIS

Our detachment was urged to prepare bottles of gasoline for defense purposes. Empty bottles were brought in bags from somewhere beyond the barricades, and there was gasoline in car gas tanks. A few of us who knew how to prepare a Molotov cocktail set about doing it. Our position was supplied with about thirty bottles, stored in holes dug for this purpose. With these weapons, we were supposed to resist the armored vehicles of the rebels.

Once again, we were due to go on duty, from 1 a.m. to 4 a.m. By this time I had observed some very alarming signs.

First, the operational command of the regiment had vanished, and the orders from the company commanders had ceased to make any strategic sense. As before, our platoon was supposed to go on duty on the barricade by the humpbacked bridge, even though no enemy was confronting us there. Everything was done as though there had been no changes in the relationship of forces, and as though we were again faced with an attack by Interior Ministry and OMON forces armed with clubs and tear gas. Meanwhile, the situation had changed fundamentally. We knew that armored vehicles were being thrown into suppressing the uprising, and that the putschists would not shrink from using live ammunition. But on an open square, we could use our Molotov cocktails only if the armored vehicles came right up to us without opening fire.

Second, there had been a noticeable decline in discipline. People were lounging around the square, some of them half-drunk, and no one was making an effort to organize them....

Worst of all was the spectacle presented by the House of Soviets. In total darkness, and with all its doors locked, the building had the air of a sarcophagus in which everyone had died or was ready to die. Rumors were circulating that hostile units of the Kantemirovskaya tank division were nearing the Supreme Soviet. Our new comrade S., assessing the situation, suggested that the platoon withdraw. He promised to shelter all twelve of us in his apartment, which was situated nearby. I supported him, arguing that they should either give us weapons now, and we would reposition ourselves for normal street fighting, or if they had forgotten about us, we should withdraw immediately. Otherwise we would share the fate of the victims of Ostankino.

The platoon commander quickly put a stop to this little mutiny....

....As the company's messenger, I went off to the headquarters. There I found a few people in uniform who urged me to have something to eat; when I refused, they sent me off to rest. There were no more orders. Those who could fight, and for whom there were enough weapons, had already decided their fate and locked themselves in the Supreme Soviet building.

(*Solidarnost* no. 23, 1993)

"YOU GUYS, LET'S HAVE A MINUTE OF SILENCE"
(transcription of radio communications on the eve of the storming of the White House. Transcribed by Ravil Zaripov. Ellipses indicate expletives deleted from newspaper account.)

The night before the storming of the White House, approximately 3:30 a.m.

Militia: You dirty rat in the White House, haven't you found a crack to hide in? Listen, in two hours your balls will be hanging on a flagpole with Khasbulatov's ass.

White House: I'd rather die here first.

M: If you don't let us sleep, we'll kill you all, starting with the Chechen and finishing with Rutskoi. Understand?

(...)

M: So what's your dirty rat keeping quiet for? Did he shove his tongue up his ass? Is our general shitting himself? And where's that bald Makashov with his flak jacket?

WH: Rats will be rats, but there's no need for this.

M: He's getting ready for the can.

M: They don't lock up corpses. Remember, no prisoners!

M: They don't take blacks in prison either.

(...)

M: You're sleeping in there, and we're talking about what to do with usurpers like Rutskoi and Khasbulatov.

M: Like the way they do it in Turkey—they'll be lying in shit with a sword hanging over their heads.

(...)

M: Look on T.V., how they beat our guys up. For that they don't just get shot, they get their skin ripped off.

M: We'll rip it off.

M: For the militia's blood, you'll pay with blood, you sons of bitches. Only criminals are hanging out there, there aren't any normal people.

M: Anyone who's hit a cop will get it from us with interest.

M: We'll hang them from the flagpoles, from every light pole.

M: It's great to talk. When's the attack going to start?

M: Not long, not long, fellas.

M: My hands are itching.

M: Don't talk about it, and it'll come sooner.

(...)

Attention all. This is the radio station of the press service of the Chief Administration of Internal Affairs. Today there were thirty-three militia casualties. Twenty-one militia members were hospitalized, eight with gunshot wounds. Two members of the Moscow militia were killed. They were Militia Lieutenant Aleksandr Ivanovich Boyko, thirty-three years old, who left a wife and two children, and Militia Colonel Ivan Dmitrievich Shishaev [the dead militia colonel's name was, in fact, Shimaev]. A militia member from 1966, and head of the criminal investigation militia in the northwest district. Rose through all the ranks. He is survived by two children, a boy and a girl, and by his wife, a schoolteacher. Today both were unarmed.

M: They'll pay for this, the sons of bitches.

M: Rutskoi will hang.

WH: Any questions, direct them to Boris Nikolayevich.

Radio Station of the Chief Administration of the Interior Ministry: The head of the guard department of the White House has disarmed all prisoners and handed them over to his fighters to be tortured.

M: Those ...!

WH: No need to swear, you guys. We've let them all go.

M: Shut up, you faggot. You'll pay for the blood of the militia with your own blood.

WH: That's how you always talk.

M: We don't just talk. We'll hang you, you ...!

M: Or else you'll get a bullet in the head.

WH: Big talkers get what they deserve. No need for that, friends.

M: We're not friends to you, scumbag. Your friends are shitting themselves, they're so scared. These are militia members talking to you, so you'd better run. Only there's nowhere for you to run. We'll get you anyway. Did you get that, half-wit, ...? And don't you swear at me.

WH: Now then, we're not swearing at you at all.

M: That's because you're a ...!

WH: No need for that, friends. That's mean.

(...)

WH: Hello, militia members. Listen, they've shown it on CNN. After the militia members gave statements, deputy Rebrikov led them out of the White House and let them go home.

M: Listen you, we've seen it all ourselves. We saw how you were shooting there, what you did to our guys. That's what we'll do to you, scumbags.

M: Who's the scumbag who's broadcasting out of the White House? Why doesn't he give his name? I want his first name and last name. I want to get together with him sometime.

M: Now guys, you know tomorrow's the Day of the Criminal Investigation Militia. Happy Criminal Investigation Militia Day.

M: You guys, can we raise a glass to the guys who got killed?

M: Only don't put it down again. To our guys who lucked out today.

M: Let's hope they're the last from our side.

WH: Let's hope they're the last in all Russia.

M: You guys, let's have a minute of silence. (On the clocks—4:10 a.m.) Pause.

This is the press service at 38 Petrovka Street. You got it. Tomorrow's the seventy-fifth birthday of criminal investigation. From 1966 Colonel Ivan Dmitrievich Shishaev [Shimaev] devoted his whole life to the fight against crime. He arrested dozens of bandits, and today he was killed while unarmed.

WH: Thirty-five of our people were killed today too.

M: And that's just the beginning.

WH: Don't be so mean, you guys. It's a sin.

M: It'll happen. You went after us with weapons, and now we're coming after you. Got it?

M: Listen, your guys weren't killed. They just died, like dogs. Why don't you stop this shit? You'd be better off coming out. Cover yourself with a white sheet and come out.

WH: If God wants it that way, I'll put on a sheet and come out.

M: You guys are already damned to hell, you rotten scumbags.

M: Attention, attention. To all members of the militia: I, a member of the militia, swear that I'll avenge our guys who got killed today. To all defenders of the White House: get ready, you creeps.

WH: There's no point in talking like that.

M: Shut your face, ape.

(...)

M: Four days, the loonies were hanging around there at Barrikadnaya. We should have stomped on them right away. Should we turn the water on or not? Let's think.

The White House, shortly after 5 p.m. on October 4.
[Photo by Vojtech Lavicka]

WH: Now guys, you're talking just like fascists.
M: Why like fascists? You've been asking for us to come and kick your head in.
(Komsomolskaya Pravda, October 13, 1993)

Machine Guns on Free Russia Square

At approximately 6:45 a.m., central Moscow was awakened by the crash of rifle and machine-gun fire. From our apartment block, located only one metro stop away, we could see about half of the House of Soviets, partly blocked from view by residential buildings. The sound of gunfire burst into the apartments, shattering the quiet of the morning. It was obvious that people were being killed. But at this time we still did not know precisely how this was occurring.

The first object to come under attack was a forward post of the White House defenders near the US Embassy, in front of the humpbacked bridge. Internal troops and civil volunteers directed automatic rifle fire on this position from armored personnel carriers which they had driven up. But no immediate assault was launched on the main barricade, reinforced with concrete blocks, which was located on the humpbacked bridge.

Several minutes later, a column of armored personnel carriers approached Free Russia Square from the opposite side, along Rochdelskaya Street. The assault force on these vehicles included armed people in civilian clothes and partial military uniform. They directed automatic rifle fire at the defenders of the barricade. Despite the gunfire, the barricade defenders attempted to set fire to the APCs with Molotov cocktails, but without success.

The evidence suggests that the attackers were not taking precise aim. But despite the early hour, the square was full of people—according to various witnesses, from 1500 to 2000 of them. As a result, the first dead and wounded began appearing. The people sleeping in the tents pitched directly on the square came under a murderous fire even before they had managed to wake up. Resistance was impossible—the supporters of the Supreme Soviet who had gathered on the square had no weapons. The most that any of the supporters of the Supreme Soviet outside the building had at their disposal was the two or three rifles and pistols in the hands of the volunteer patrol that from time to time went around the barricades.

People began to seek refuge. Some ran into the White House, some lay down directly on the square, and some tried to take cover in the two-story auxiliary building. Bullets caught people in the back as they fled. People were cut down in the vestibules of the ground floor of the House of Soviets, as the entrances came under crossfire.

Mixed with the clatter of rifle fire was a louder booming sound which hammered on people's ears even three kilometers away. This came from the heavy-caliber machine guns in the turrets of the armored vehicles. Bursts from these machine guns cut to ribbons the tents in which unarmed defenders of the House of Soviets had spent the night, tore heads from bodies, and literally ripped people in half. Soon, armored vehicles appeared from the side of the humpbacked bridge as well. They too opened fire. The situation of the unarmed people became hopeless.

The crowd poured off the square, carrying away the wounded. Dozens of corpses remained lying on the ground. How many were there, these first victims of the shooting? The first journalists on the scene of the tragedy after the assault spoke of some twenty to thirty bodies lying on the square and in the ditch beneath the humpbacked bridge.

The official version claimed that the armored personnel carriers that approached the building of the Supreme Soviet were fired on by its defenders and were forced to open return fire on the building. The official media maintained a complete silence on the way the attackers fired on the unarmed crowd in front of the building. Refusing completely to touch upon this topic, they would not even condescend to deny the charges made in eyewitness reports published in several newspapers. Witnesses state that there was no shooting from the House of Soviets, and that the armored vehicles were not responding to fire from the building, but were shooting at the people on the square. They opened fire on the building of the House of Soviets only after the defenders of the Supreme Soviet had left the square.

By approximately 8 a.m., the House of Soviets was ringed from all sides by armored personnel carriers (wheeled vehicles each armed with a heavy-caliber machine gun) and BMP-2 armored vehicles, which have caterpillar tracks and are armed with automatic cannon. The attackers began firing continuously on the lower floors of the building. Here there were large areas of glass, and bullets could readily penetrate from one side of the structure almost to the other. Mounting return fire was almost impossible—anyone who attempted this would come under massive fire, not only from the armored vehicles, but also from snipers on the roofs of nearby apartment blocks, in the mayor's office, and in the Hotel Mir. Moreover, Rutskoi had issued an order forbidding anyone to shoot back.

The three floors of the mayor's office occupied by supporters of Rutskoi were cleaned out quickly by a massive fusillade that turned them into a sieve. These floors were engulfed in flame. The people in the building who remained alive had no chance of putting up resistance.

The assault was drawing to a close.

Interview with Aleksandr Strakhov (obtained by Andrei Kolganov)
Were there any soldiers there?
There were only civilians, no soldiers at all. There were people in helmets, a few had bulletproof vests, and some had shields, but these people were civilians. Where had they gotten this special equipment? From my recollection, and from what people were saying, it had been abandoned by the OMON the previous day, or taken from them.

I stress this, because at about 7 a.m., people by the humpbacked bridge heard automatic rifle fire—from some distance off. It wasn't close, but they heard it. People began to jump up from their places. This was between the White House, the iron fence of the park, and the humpbacked bridge. After ten minutes or less, armored personnel carriers approached from the other side, and partitioned off the narrow corridor between the House of Soviets and the high fence of the park. I saw women approach these armored personnel carriers. A few minutes later, bursts of automatic fire began coming from that direction. The troops had begun firing from these vehicles. At first they were shooting from automatic rifles. Initially, some people lay down, but then they leapt up and began running, as it had become clear that this wasn't simply a random burst of fire. The attackers had obviously begun shooting the whole place up, in deadly seriousness. After this, they began shooting out of heavy-caliber machine guns. At first, people tried to take shelter behind the two-story building on the side of the humpbacked bridge. But when shooting began from the side of the humpbacked bridge, and armored personnel carriers appeared there, people were told to get inside the building. It was at this moment, after shooting had already begun from the armored personnel carriers, that I saw people with guns for the first time.

And while all this was going on, people were firing from inside the White House on the armored personnel carriers and the people in them?

No. No, it was all one-sided. Everyone was fleeing from danger—from the shooting that was coming from the armored personnel carriers. If they'd had to shelter from fire coming from the White House, it would have been completely logical for them to have run to the wall of the White House itself. Here they would have been completely protected if anyone were firing at them from above, since there's an overhang. But the people were running from the armored vehicles, since that's where the fire was coming from. I particularly recall a burst of fire that destroyed a streetlight on a pole near the humpbacked bridge. It was blown completely to pieces—that was from a machine gun, not an automatic rifle. It wasn't small-arms fire, it was from a heavy-caliber machine gun.

It was after the shooting had begun that I saw people with weapons for the first time. They were most likely people who'd come from the House of Soviets. Before this, all the doors and entrances had been closed. I didn't see anyone going either to or from the building. These people said to get inside the two-story building and go up to the top floor. There was a child screaming there, a child literally one or two years old, and no one could quiet it. People were already wounded. At first we went into a windowless room where the machine-gun bullets probably wouldn't penetrate. But then we heard small-caliber cannon fire, not from the armored personnel carriers, but from the BMP-2s....

Automatic cannon?

Yes, yes. We were already in the building. The people who had weapons—there were three with automatic rifles and eight with pistols—tried to get the unarmed civilians, of whom there were a lot, out of this danger zone. There were hundreds of people. In effect, it was everyone who'd managed to flee from the square when the shooting started. They broke two windows that opened onto the park. The two-story building stands right on the line of the fence, and the windows open directly onto the park. They tried to get people out through these windows, but it didn't work—the park was being fired on. At the first attempt, they started shooting from the direction of the park.

After this everyone who was there, old and young, crawled across the zone that was under fire, since the small building was being riddled with bullets. There was shooting from the automatic rifles, and from the cannon. At first I thought this was machine-gun fire, but the rate of fire is a little less. We began taking people down below into a bomb shelter. It was a big place with seven-meter ceilings and massive doors closing off the entrances, like in the metro. People began sitting around there. Two people in military uniform—I think they were colonels—began handing out gas masks, because people were saying there'd probably be a gas attack. We picked out gas masks for the old women, screwed filters onto them, put in non-fogging film, and in general showed them how to use them. There were a lot of women there.

(Tape-recorded testimony)

Interview with Vojtech Lavicka, photojournalist, citizen of the Czech Republic. Obtained by Andrei Kolganov.

Did you see unarmed people in front of the White House when the shooting began?

No, because I missed the first moments. When I came out onto the balcony, all I saw was armored personnel carriers firing on the White House. I was told later that some of the people scattered, while others ran into the two-story building and into the entrances to the White House. There they lay on the floor to try to save themselves from the shooting. I personally saw wounded people there, who were carried off. I was told that some of the wounded who were in the two-story building were later taken by an underground passage to the White House and placed in a primitive hospital there.

(Tape-recorded testimony)

Anatoliy Nabatov, artist
BULLET-RIDDLED PEOPLE, BULLET-RIDDLED PICTURES
Testimony of an eyewitness

I was asleep when the first shots rang out. Bullets immediately struck the place where I usually sat at the table. In front of my eyes, the canvases of two paintings were punctured by a burst of machine-gun fire.

Despite pleas to get out of the room quickly, a deputy who had been sleeping on a table began to gather his socks that had dried

Civilians waiting on the mezzanine for an opportunity to go out around 3 p.m. on October 4, following rumors of a government decision to send the Alpha anti-terrorist unit to make an exit corridor for civilians. All afternoon, unarmed civilians waited unsuccessfully for an opportunity to leave.

[Photo by Vojtech Lavicka]

overnight—he'd washed them the night before and hung them up to dry. But when a few bullets slammed into the cupboard above his head, he made a leap for the door. On the square in front of the White House the unimaginable was happening. In various places there, as many as a thousand people had been gathered in small groups. Some people had been warming themselves at campfires, while others had been asleep in tents. These people were the first victims—there were a lot of women and children among them. People who managed to run through the doors of the White House were hit by bullets coming through the huge glass windows of the ground floor lobby.

(*Pravda,* December 21, 1993)

The View from Inside

Around eight o'clock in the morning, squads of attackers rushed into the ground floor of the House of Soviets through its numerous entrances. By this time, the area had been shredded by automatic cannon fire. The covering forces of the guard and of volunteer defenders in these entrances were quickly dealt with. One group of attackers burst into the building through the basement. The wounded who had been evacuated there, along with some of the unarmed supporters and staff of the Supreme Soviet, found themselves in the midst of a firefight.

The bottom two floors of the six-floor structure forming the broad base of the House of Soviets were quickly captured. But in the tall central section of the building, the wave of attackers encountered organized resistance.

It was in this section of the building, above the second floor, that most of the unarmed supporters of the Supreme Soviet, the members of its staff, the service personnel, and the people's deputies were situated. They were in the chamber of the Soviet of Nationalities of the Supreme Soviet, to which the gunfire was not penetrating from outside, and in the corridors of the third, fourth, and fifth floors. These floors were partly protected from the heavy weapons fire because they were surrounded by the "box" of the six-floor section of the building. Higher than this, civilians were not permitted to go; there it was much more dangerous.

The first wave of attackers consisted of subunits of the OMON, Interior Ministry special forces troops, and volunteers who had served in the Afghan war. Over the radio, the defenders of the House of Soviets could hear how the attackers were pledging to annihilate them all, not to take prisoners, and so forth. They knew what these "defenders of democracy" had done at Ostankino, and how they had just dealt with the unarmed people on the square. Everyone, armed and unarmed, was determined to fight to the death.

The people concentrated here were not a motley group of volunteers, but members of the Union of Officers, somewhere between two hundred and fifty and three hundred people. They directed a withering fire against the invaders who were trying to break through onto the second floor from below by way of the main staircases. The attackers were not ready for this. It was one thing for them to shoot down unarmed people, but it was quite another to climb up in the face of bullets. They quickly backtracked, abandoning their dead and wounded.

No more such attacks were tried. The final cleansing of the captured part of the building was carried out by squads of the Interior Ministry special forces and by airborne troops. They slowly forced the relatively few defenders out of one floor after another, until all six floors were taken. Then the invaders tried to burst into the central part of the House of Soviets, using a tactic that involved numerous groups attacking simultaneously from many directions. But the defenders, who had blocked the corridors with barricades of safes and metal cabinets, stubbornly fought off the attack.

Among the unarmed people who were gathered in the White House were many young men who had had military training, and among the pensioners were retired military officers. They demanded repeatedly that the people in charge of the defense distribute weapons to them, but this was refused. For every fighter with an automatic rifle, there were thus five unarmed people lined up, waiting for the chance to take over the weapon if the fighter were killed.

By midday the onslaught had weakened, and only from time to time were there exchanges of fire within the building. The snipers surrounding the White House shot at any target that presented itself. Firing continued from heavy machine guns and automatic cannon of various types; from around 11 a.m. on, they were joined by four tanks.

As a tactical element in the assault on the building, the artillery bombardment of the upper floors was pointless. It was a pure act of terrorism, designed to show that the ruling clique which had carried out the coup d'etat would stop at nothing in order to defend its power.

The military subunits around the House of Soviets obviously had no burning wish to press ahead with the assault on the building, sacrificing their lives for the sake of Yeltsin and his team. After midday, the first negotiations began. Earlier, Rutskoi and the other people leading the defense had appealed repeatedly to the forces storming the White House, calling on them to allow the evacuation of noncombatants, among whom were many women and children. Foreign embassies, including that of the United States, were informed of this situation. But the appeals were not honored with a reply.

It was only after midday that negotiations with the White House were opened. The first proposal was that anyone who wanted to come out should do so under a white flag. This sounded like a grim joke—come out under incessant artillery and machine-gun fire? No one gave any guarantees, or even promised to stop shooting. Another proposal came from one of the junior commanders of the airborne troops; he undertook to have his forces bring unarmed people out of the building. Unfortunately, he could not guarantee that the attackers would cease fire. The civilians inside the building were united in refusing to come out under such conditions.

Several attempts to hold talks were thwarted because truce envoys with white flags could not leave the building in the face of incessant fire. One of the daring individuals who nevertheless decided to do this was killed before the eyes of the White House defenders. Another envoy, a journalist from the agency Postfactum, who had been sent at the request of Rutskoi, reported in an article for the newspaper *Izvestiya* that he had been arrested on the ground floor by defenders of the White House who regarded him with excessive suspicion. No doubt these were the journalist's personal impressions. But by this time, the first two floors of the House of Soviets had long since been captured by the airborne and special forces troops, and no defenders of the White House could have been there.

Finally, talks with the commanders of the airborne detachments began. As a result, the airborne troops ceased fire, turned their armored vehicles so that the barrels were pointed away from the House of Soviets (this could be seen in the CNN newscast), and sent unarmed negotiators into the interior of the House of Soviets to organize the evacuation of noncombatants. Bringing about a general ceasefire was more difficult. The tank detachments continued their shelling despite repeated appeals. A small group of young people nevertheless left the building, moving under fire in short rushes. But for many hundreds of women and elderly people, such an escape was out of the question.

During the afternoon, the President of the Ingush Republic, Ruslan Aushev, and the President of Kalmykiya, Kirsan Ilyumzhinov, managed to penetrate the House of Soviets on a peace mission. They also offered to act as intermediaries in evacuating noncombatants. The defenders of the White House told them that they were ready to lay down their arms in order to avoid further bloodshed, provided there were at least minimal guarantees against quick reprisals.

Such guarantees were essential, since around 1 or 2 p.m. several unarmed daredevils managed to enter the House of Soviets, and reported to the defenders that the first prisoners to be captured were being subjected to beatings and taunts from the militia, the OMON, and the pro-Yeltsin crowd.

Late in the afternoon on October 4. Above, the man on the right, a priest, had been in the White House since September 21. In a makeshift chapel, he took confessions and held services twice a day. Below, civilians waiting to go out.
[Photo by Vojtech Lavicka]

A similar fate befell Ilyumzhinov's bodyguards and members of a peace mission who were arrested by special forces troops in the cordon.

By 4 p.m., members of the special antiterrorist Alpha group had entered the building, and also declared their readiness to ensure that noncombatants and people who laid down their arms were able to leave.

The shooting finally stopped, and the first groups of besieged people began leaving the building.

Interview with Aleksandr Strakhov (obtained by Andrei Kolganov)

We could hear that an intense battle was raging up above. Volunteers had begun to carry dead and wounded people through this basement area; now the flow accelerated sharply. After a while someone gave the order to stand up and move in a body through the huge doorway, keeping to the left wall. First of all, naturally, they let women and children through. In single file, one after the other, they led us through the underground corridors. Further on, there was no light, everything was completely dark. It was a real bomb shelter. Along the corridors were wooden bunks and ventilators. It should be understood that by the time they started taking us out, it had become very difficult to breathe. There were a lot of people, and despite the large space it had become hard to breathe, because the electricty was turned off and the ventilation wasn't working. For a considerable time we walked in complete darkness, with only a few pocket flashlights. Each of us put a hand on the shoulder of the person in front, and that was how we went. The column stretched out for hundreds of meters. Again and again we went down, climbed up, and went around corners.

Finally we sensed that it had become easier to breathe. Up above was a staircase, with what reminded me of the normal wire mesh around the staircase of an apartment building. We were in a basement room of the House of Soviets, a long room of a hundred square meters or even more. In the distance was a bend, and we could see the doors of elevators, fire shields—it was an ordinary basement. There were a lot of people there, standing or sitting along all the walls; only a narrow walkway remained. Then people in military uniforms appeared. They were armed, or at least, a lot of them had weapons. There were perhaps twenty people with automatic rifles.

I want to stress that neither before, during, nor after all this did anyone hand out weapons to other people. Or, to be more precise, I didn't see anyone handing out weapons, and didn't hear of it being done. As for weapons simply being given out, or distributed on the basis of student cards—nothing of the kind happened.

When we were told that the attackers were breaking through, if they hadn't broken through already, along the passageway by which we'd come, the people with guns began leading the others out in groups of ten, while themselves taking cover. We were taken up the staircases to the corridors on the third, fourth, and fifth floors. There it seemed safer, and subsequently this turned out to be true. Later, there was a gas attack and shooting in the basement.

The staircases were all under fire, and the people with guns led us up, I stress, while taking cover. The shooting was practically nonstop. I was first on the second floor, and then on the third. There were huge numbers of people—the corridors were filled to overflowing. It was the same on every floor. If there were two hundred people in the corridor on each floor, then you could work out the total number with a fair degree of accuracy. We learned that people were jammed in like that on five floors.

How many people were there in all, by your estimate?

If there were two hundred people in our corridor alone, then multiplying by five you get a figure of about a thousand. I wouldn't venture to estimate how many dead and wounded there were—this is virtually impossible to work out for a whole series of reasons. But there were a lot of people there, and I stress once again that all these people were unarmed civilians.

Were people very scared?

Extremely. How's someone supposed to feel when they're unarmed, when they might never have seen a gun in their life, and suddenly they start getting machine-gunned on this square! If they'd just warned us: "Get out of the way, we're going to start shooting!" Though even then they wouldn't have been justified. But there was nothing like that—without a word, they just started shooting people on this so-called Free Russia Square.

People were naturally very afraid. The women were very scared to go upstairs from the basement. But it was already clear that it was even more dangerous to remain there than to go upstairs. Who could have predicted what was going to happen after that? No one would even have dreamed of it in a nightmare.

Who did we see there with weapons? They were people in military uniform, in bulletproof vests and helmets. I should probably say something about the people who, I later discovered, are called Barkashovites. I saw people there in a sort of uniform, with red badges sewn onto the sleeves. To tell the truth, this was the first time I'd seen either the people or the emblems. I wasn't paying particular attention to them at that time. I didn't know who the people were or what the badges signified. They weren't armed. They were relatively young, twenty-five years or less, and they were also on our floor. They were completely unarmed. I should say, though, that there was one person there with a firearm, though he wasn't one of the Barkashovites. If you could call it a firearm—it was a beautiful-looking hunting rifle which, the man admitted, wouldn't fire. It's clear enough what kind of impact a gun has when it's not in working order—purely psychological. The man with this gun was twenty-two years old.

In a word, the Barkashovites were unarmed. They were of various ages, but mainly young.

There was a portable radio transmitter next to me, on which we could hear conversations. Whether these were milita members or soldiers talking, I can't say. We listened to these conversations until the batteries started to run down, and the signal was audible only intermittently. Somewhere around eleven or twelve o'clock, by my guess, or perhaps only ten o'clock (it was hard to keep track of time, since we were in a windowless corridor where there was no light—further along there were corridors where there were windows, so only the ends of our corridor were lit up) they began shooting with guns that weren't just small-caliber cannon. Loud reports echoed all over, and the walls began to shake.

There I met someone I knew, who had come down from the sixth floor. An incendiary shell had hit there, and a fire had begun. We were indescribably happy that we were both alive. It was just understood—there was no need for words. It was explained to us that they'd begun firing from tanks. It was impossible to understand this from our point of view, and I still don't understand it. You can explain it, but you still can't understand it—how could they be shooting out of tanks at unarmed people, who not only couldn't shoot back, but who didn't have any weapons.... You shouldn't just shoot people, in any circumstances!

Did these unarmed people try to surrender?

After the tanks started shooting, even old grandfathers began going up to the soldiers who were guarding the staircases and windows and asking them for weapons, even begging them tearfully. They were saying, "Give us weapons, we don't want to be shot like pheasants. Give us weapons, we don't have anything to lose." But they still didn't give anyone guns. They came up to the man with the hunting rifle and asked him for his gun. He answered, "Take it, only it doesn't shoot."

From time to time women brought water, and someone brought crackers. People divided up whatever there was. Several times, deputies came in and told us not to worry, they were doing everything possible to get us out of the White House. Deputies came there many times. Of the ones I knew by sight, I particularly remember seeing Svetlana Goryacheva, and a certain colonel—I'd seen many of them on television, but I didn't remember their names. They came up many times and told us not to worry, they'd get us out. As confirmation of this, I can say that I heard on the portable radio how Rutskoi declared that he, Acting President of the Russian Federation Aleksandr Vladimirovich Rutskoi, called on them to name the doorway through which truce envoys could come out, so as to negotiate the safe passage of a large number of unarmed people, women and children, who were inside the building. After that, he said, they could do as they liked with the rest of the people inside the House of Soviets, only they should allow unarmed people to leave. Rutskoi repeated this many times, and Abdulatipov later made similar appeals over the radio.

Time passed. There was a certain period when the shooting died down, but then it started up again. Over the portable radio, we heard repeatedly that a column of armored personnel carriers was approaching from a particular direction. Then the column seemed to have been lost; what could have happened to the twelve armored personnel carriers? Twelve armored personnel carriers were urgently needed at the White House. Then someone said that a column was on its way, twenty-eight vehicles as I remember. Then for a considerable time there were uninterrupted conversations about a column of ninety armored personnel carriers; people were saying that they didn't know what type these were. How were the commanders to know whose side the vehicles were on...?

The shooting continued. People were becoming very tense, and then relaxing a little, thinking that some kind of help was coming that would end all this. Then the shooting began again, and again people's hopes evaporated. Somewhere around 3:30 or 4:00, after some kind of talks had taken place, a man in civilian clothes suddenly appeared. He was dressed in a leather jacket and carrying a folder; he introduced himself as a colonel. A captain appeared, in a bulletproof vest and without weapons. According to the colonel, the captain was from the airborne regiment, and had been sent by his side to try to reach agreement on some way of getting people out. When people heard this, they all jumped up from their places, shouting that they didn't believe it, that the troops outside had already been firing at them point-blank for many hours. The captain could see for himself what kind of red-brown bandits were inside the building—and so forth. They didn't believe the promises—that was the gist of it.

And in fact, anyone who had gone out under fire, who had tried to leave, had been shot on the spot. People had seen through the windows how the troops outside were firing on people, how they were shooting people down. They had seen how a soldier with a white flag had gone to try to negotiate, and had been shot. It was said that another truce envoy had been killed as well. This was directly beneath our windows, by the staircase and the end of our corridor.

Then a decision was made to leave the White House and to try to reach agreement with the commanders of the attacking forces on getting people out. As someone who isn't so old, and who likes to think of himself as sensible and able to persuade others, I volunteered to go to the airborne troops and to try to reach agreement on how to bring about a ceasefire and how to get people out.

Strange as it may seem, two young people volunteered to go with me—a sixteen-year-old woman and a man of twenty-one. Together with them, and with this captain, I went through the basement, which was largely covered in blood. Everything there was strewn all over the floor, helmets and bulletproof vests had been thrown everywhere, and there were people there as well. We went out through the ground floor....

You mentioned people. Do you mean people who'd been killed?

Yes, there were dead bodies there, too. I can't say there were a lot of them, but there was a lot of blood on the floor, and a lot of bulletproof vests and helmets had been dropped there. It's not hard to imagine.... When we went down there, it smelled of gas. There had been a gas attack there, and you could see that they'd sprayed the place with bursts of gunfire. It was obvious what this was going to lead to—the results were all over the floor. The walls there were concrete, and wherever you fired, you were going to hit something.

Multiple ricochet?

Yes, multiple ricochet. And there were a lot of steel doors there. When we went through the ground floor, almost all the doors were open, everything was in total disorder, the windows were all broken and had bullet-holes in them, and on the tables everything had been overturned as though people had been looking for something. The telephones and computers had been smashed. When we went out through a broken window of the first floor (to understand what I mean, if you stand on the embankment side facing the central entrance, then on the staircase side, that is on the right, below the ground floor, there are dirt slopes—this is behind the access road for vehicles going to the central entrance), we came out just by the right-hand corner of the building. A large number of soldiers were there, and two armored vehicles from the airborne regiment. What I saw there was very strange—150 people, or at any rate more than a hundred, were sitting on the ground, in military uniform, without weapons, and without bulletproof vests. This surprised me.

Next to the armored vehicle stood soldiers of the airborne regiment, in bulletproof vests, with weapons, with sniper rifles, and with automatic weapons of various types. The captain started looking for the commander of the regiment, and in the end we found him....

....It took a long time to find the commander of the regiment, somewhere around half an hour. People tried repeatedly to drive us away, but we didn't leave. We stood arm in arm—the young man, the young woman, and I. People left us alone only when the colonel and the captain who had come with us said that we had come from the White House to conduct talks. The shooting was continuing. Then the commander of the regiment appeared, and over a two-way radio ordered that the firing cease, though for a long time it didn't die down. They were shooting in the area of the far right-hand corner of the building, near the humpbacked bridge. It was clear that they were shooting out of cannon and machine guns, and that bullets were ricocheting off the walls.

When we came out, we were shocked to look at the White House. There wasn't a single window intact, not one. This was true not just of the lower part of the building, but also of the tower. It was clear that there'd been a fire in the central part of the tower. The shelling from the tanks resumed, and before our eyes, a fire broke out in the upper part of the tower.

The commander of the regiment appeared, and the shooting ceased—but not for long, perhaps for five minutes. Then it started up again. No one was shooting from inside the White House, while from outside there was gunfire both from cannon and from machine guns. The commander of the regiment sent an officer to the far right-hand corner, because they hadn't responded in any way on the two-way radio to the instructions to cease fire. The shooting stopped, but five minutes later it began again. A second officer was sent, this very same captain, the company commander. His surname was Vasilyev, or perhaps Vasilchikov, and he was a young man of perhaps twenty-seven. He returned with a bleeding hand, after being hit by a shell splinter. He brought some splinters with him. The shooting didn't come to an end for a long time, and then only when this captain ran off there once again.

While we were by the building, gunshots rang out from the Hotel Mir, from the side of the mayor's office. The snipers who were near us looked at the hotel through their telescopic sights as if taking aim, but didn't fire.

I was struck by the fact that the airborne troops at this corner deliberately turned the weapons of the armored vehicles away from the building, and pointed the barrels upward. No one fired out of them. When shots rang out, the troops tried to take cover behind the ramp and behind the armored vehicles, but didn't fire. They said they'd had forty people killed. I asked them how that could have been. "Snipers were shooting from over there," they said, pointing to the hotel. I was staggered to learn this, since, as they explained to us, the mayor's office was at this stage occupied by supporters of the former president, and had been for a long time. Who could have been shooting from the building with a sniper rifle, you could only guess.

I've been a soldier myself, and I saw sniper rifles in the hands of those airborne troops. But I personally didn't see a single sniper rifle in the hands of the armed people inside the House of Soviets. Nor were there any machine guns, such as were shown later on television. There were

Kalashnikov automatic rifles, and Makarov and Stechkin pistols. In general there were very few people with firearms. In the stairwell next to the floor where I'd sheltered, there were two or three people with guns—one or two with automatic rifles, and one or two with pistols.

But wouldn't most of those who were armed have been in the line of fire?

They were firing from everywhere, though of course most of the people who had weapons were at the points where the attackers were breaking through to the interior, and this was understandable. But there were no vast crowds of armed people. The only weapons were in the hands of a few people in the stairwell.

We gave the commander of the regiment the materials we'd brought with us. Before leaving the building, we'd gone around the floors and explained to people that here we were, unarmed, going out to hold talks with the airborne troops to get them to stop shooting. All the unarmed people would line up in the corridors and be led out of the House of Soviets. After this we went outside. I handed over what I'd brought to the commander of the regiment, and explained everything to him. He said, right, now we'll cease fire, let's agree on how and where we'll bring the people out. We agreed that they'd come out through that entrance, right there.

Once we'd gone back into the building, the shooting resumed. And when we were inside, we continued hearing numerous shots. It was easy to distinguish the shooting that was coming from outside, since there were no heavy-caliber weapons inside, and couldn't have been. We had no trouble telling where the shots were coming from. We went into the building—I myself, the young man and woman, the captain, and along with him three more people. They included the colonel in civilian clothes, and a tall, relatively young man of about forty, in civilian clothes, who described himself as a representative of the trade union at the ZiL car factory. This man actively attached himself to us, wanting to go in with us and bring the people out. So we set off, without weapons, with a two-way radio, after agreeing that if we didn't come out within an hour, it would mean that additional efforts would have to be made to bring about a ceasefire.

Staying together in this group we went along the floors, in order to assemble all the unarmed people and lead them out of the building. As we went along we naturally kept shouting out that we'd come from the negotiations, that we were truce envoys, and that people shouldn't shoot. On one of the stairwell landings there were two soldiers in special forces uniforms. They had helmets equipped with visors and built-in two-way radios, and were armed with automatic rifles. They demanded that the captain show them his documents. He introduced himself as a company commander, named his unit, and showed them his military ID card; they in turn showed their documents. When the second of them—not the one who was checking the documents—heard that I and two others had been inside the building earlier, he pressed his rifle to my throat and said: "So that means it's you who killed my Serega? I'll spread you all over the wall!"

After we'd gone around the floors, and climbed the stairs to the top floor, we saw two people there who were probably about sixty years old. They were in civilian clothes, but had helmets, as well as bulletproof vests which they'd put on awkwardly over their jackets. They were armed with automatic rifles. I imagined they were deputies or members of the staff. They didn't shoot, and when we explained what we were doing, they let us through.

Do you have any information, or any personal impressions, about how the fighting went inside the House of Soviets?

The people from outside had a massive advantage, that was absolutely clear. It was also quite clear that they didn't stand on ceremony, and shot at anyone they set eyes on, armed or unarmed, without discrimination. The proof of that was the large number of dead, including elderly people and adolescents. I'd single out in particular the soldiers of the Tamanskaya division, who were totally unable to calm themselves down, and who were constantly starting up shooting. On the other hand, I'd like to say another word in favor of the airborne troops, who told us they were from Naro-Fominsk. I repeat that no one in the White House handed out weapons to anyone, even when they asked for them. Old people in particular were begging: "Give us weapons, we don't want to be shot like pheasants!"

It still rankles with me: why were the people who were there described as red-browns, bandits, rebels, and so forth, when what actually happened is that many of them were shot down for their beliefs—unarmed people. It's not right to shoot unarmed people whatever their thinking. Not even if they're fascists, and all the people who were there are being linked for some reason with fascism.

Rutskoi and Khasbulatov were there. Did they make any effort to go among the people, to organize them in some way, to reassure them?

I saw Rutskoi down in the basement, when they brought us into the basement through underground passageways. From what I understand, he was there to assess for himself the danger that the attackers would get into the basement through these passageways. He gave the order to get the civilians out of the basement, since there they could all be shot literally with a couple of bursts of automatic fire. As I said, I personally heard Rutskoi make repeated appeals over the radio for the other side to name an exit through which envoys could come out and negotiate the safe passage of a large number of unarmed people, women and children, who were in the building. After this, the attackers could deal with the rest of the people as they chose. These are Rutskoi's words, as I heard them over the radio.

Did the soldiers who were outside regard what was happening as proper?

No. For example, when we went out past the airborne troops, who were formed up in a corridor, they didn't even hold their rifles ready. They acted in the same spirit as earlier, when they'd raised the barrels of the guns in their armored vehicles.

A girlfriend of my daughter's was killed near the White House—she and a friend had gone to drag away the wounded. She was around fifteen to seventeen years old.... And among those who were killed.... [Here Strakhov could no longer speak. A pause]

Was it really for the sake of this that our generation in effect gave up everything? So they could shoot us and our children? We weren't threatening anyone, in any way. I wasn't threatening anyone—I didn't have a gun in my hands. I've already said how I'd characterize this—it's fascism. I don't know how else you'd describe it.

I can recount a lot of testimonies from eyewitnesses. For example, how they were catching snipers. There was an old woman who heard shots coming from above her apartment. She came down and said, "You're looking for snipers—there's a couple of them sitting up above me." And they told her, "We know about them, they're ours." There are testimonies from residents in nearby buildings who are ready to swear to this in court. There are a lot of testimonies about what happened in neighboring streets and courtyards....

There are recordings of radio conversations. They were recorded not just in one place, but in several. They were taped in the White House, in the offices of the Moscow Soviet, and by private individuals and various official functionaries as well. There were dozens of hours of tape recordings. All this has to be put in front of people, so they can judge for themselves.

You wanted to say something more about the weapons....

According to a large number of testimonies, including some by people I know personally, people were given weapons after they'd signed a contract, that is, after they'd signed on for real military service. The legal authorities had a perfect right to do this. It was called the First Special Motorized Infantry Regiment. These people really were given weapons, but there were very few of them.

(Tape-recorded testimony)

Interview with Vojtech Lavicka, photojournalist, citizen of the Czech Republic. Obtained by Andrei Kolganov.

I came late at night to the White House, and spent the night there in a separate room with other journalists, in total darkness. Around 7:30, we were awakened by gunshots. I went down below, cautiously went out onto the balcony, and saw three armored personnel carriers that were firing on the White House.

We went back into the building. The shooting continued. About ten o'clock, as we were going along a corridor which was under fire from snipers, one of the bullets wounded a colleague, a journalist from Interfax. She was wounded in the leg. We carried her off to a first aid station, where they bandaged her. She remained with us all day, and left with us.

Sometime before twelve, other journalists and I went around various floors. Then they sent us back from the fifth floor when we tried to go higher. They told us we couldn't go there, so we went back down. Somewhere about this time, the radio in the building announced that the deputies were gathering in the parliamentary chamber, which is behind the main staircase. We went down there as well. We encountered a huge crowd of people. There were deputies present, and many of the people who weren't involved in the defense of the building also went down there. There were cleaners, service personnel, workers from the buffet—just a mass of people. I'd say there were many hundreds of people,

Unarmed teenage boys on the second floor of the White House, around 4:45 p.m. on October 4, on the side of the building under fire from tanks and snipers, walking through with an armored shield. A number of children were trapped inside the building.

[Photo by Vojtech Lavicka]

perhaps seven hundred to a thousand. These were civilians who had nothing to do with the defense of the building, and who'd gathered in this place because there were people there, and it was possible to get some kind of information.

From time to time I walked about the building, even though it was under fire. The corridors ended in large windows, through which stray bullets were constantly flying and into which snipers were firing. It was quite dangerous. In one of the rooms a sort of shrine had been set up; a priest and an icon were there, and people came to pray.

There were several first aid stations. On the various floors I saw three first aid stations that had been set up in offices. People were bandaged, put on IV tubes and so forth while lying on the tables. I spoke with one first aid worker who said that the largest first aid station, or hospital, was on the ground floor, and that several dozen dead and several dozen wounded were there.

From about 1 p.m. on, deputies started going around the building, saying that they were in contact with the government and with various authorities and were trying to reach agreement on how to get people out. I personally spoke with Iona Andronov, who said there was an agreement that both sides would stop firing and that all these people would leave. Oleg Rumyantsev also said he was in contact with various officials, that it was rather difficult, but that he'd finally gotten through to the prime minister, who had also promised him that the people would be able to leave. Around two o'clock, Ruslan Khasbulatov appeared in a corridor. He talked with people, and sat for a while on a windowsill. He was seriously worried. He wasn't in a state of depression, but he was very concerned. Everyone understood that the situation was serious, and that something had to be done for these unarmed people.

Somewhere around two o'clock, it was announced that agreement had been reached with the Alpha group. They were to ensure that firing stopped from their side, and were to organize a corridor through which people could leave. People began gathering at the main staircase on the embankment side. Several hundred people were there—women with shopping bags, and children, even very young ones. It was even said that there was a two-year-old, though I didn't see this child myself. I saw children of five or six. I was told that women who worked there had nowhere to leave their children, so they brought them to work. I saw a blind man walking with a stick. There were large numbers of people of military age who were unarmed.

I spoke with OMON members who had been guarding the bridge and who had been beaten up on October 3. When the crowd marched on October 3 from Oktyabrskaya Square to the Foreign Ministry, these OMON members had been standing there as a covering force. They said some interesting things—that their weapons had been taken away, and that they'd been very tired, since they'd been on duty for several days in a row. When the crowd marched towards them, they received an order to withdraw. When they came in contact with the crowd they were unprepared, waiting for someone to lead them away, so they were easily defeated. At first they weren't given any orders, but then they were told to go to the mayor's office. When the mayor's office also came under attack, they found themselves effectively trapped. On orders from their superiors, they'd come to the White House—a group of fifty people, without defensive gear. "We don't know what we're supposed to be doing here," they said. "We're sitting here because there's simply nowhere for us to go."

There were also people there who'd come to defend the White House, but who weren't armed, and who were more or less superfluous. I spoke with former officers who said they'd come there to fight, but hadn't been given weapons—they'd been given only one Kalashnikov rifle for twelve people. They said they were irrelevant, that there was nothing for them to do. From this I understood that weapons were in short supply, and the talk about weapons being given out to everyone strikes me as completely implausible. Those who received weapons were mainly soldiers who wanted to fight.

Ruslan Khasbulatov then went upstairs to his office. The people remained below. Eventually, various people came in, parliamentarians who said they had an agreement and would lead people out. Several groups of ten or twenty people left. For example, someone came in, gathered a group of twenty people, and left through entrance twenty-four. With them went a colleague of mine, who said that they went out across a space that was under fire, and that was being fired on even as they left. That is, they were under fire, running, and trying to take cover. It was possible for some people, the younger ones who could run, to get out. But as for bringing out old women who couldn't run, and a crowd of six hundred people.... Three people might run across, but a hundred or two hundred wouldn't make it.

Everyone was waiting for the Alpha group to come and form a corridor through which it would be possible to leave more or less safely. But as soon as a small group started off, the shooting began once more. So people would rush in the appropriate direction, the shooting would begin, and then everyone would run back. There were times when we thought we'd go. Then no, we wouldn't go. Then again we'd go, and then no, we wouldn't....

Around three o'clock, a situation arose that I thought was quite dangerous. For a while the shooting stopped, and some strange people appeared down below in the vestibule. There had been shooting all around, and suddenly, here were these young men in jackets, white shirts, and ties, and carrying briefcases. It wasn't clear where they'd come from or who'd let them through. The guards, who were standing up above since they no longer held the ground floor, yelled out: "What are you doing here? Get away!" The men replied: "We've come to observe."

It's also strange that as well as these men, there were others in athletic jackets. They were very reminiscent of the guys who usually guard kiosks. Well-developed young men, with bulging muscles. At times we heard pistol shots down below. It wasn't clear who was shooting at whom, or why.

All this was very dangerous. It seemed like a reconnaissance mission—as though these people had come to observe what was happening, what the mood was like. At any moment a detachment of shock troops might follow them, or they themselves might suddenly start shooting or throwing grenades. It was dangerous because there was a crowd of unarmed people. If shooting broke out, the people would run, they'd be hit by stray bullets, and it would be a massacre.

Just at this time, some people managed to get into the building from outside. They told us that a crowd of Yeltsin supporters were waiting, and were searching and beating up anyone who got out. If you got out, you were still far from safe—once you'd managed to leave, you were in this crowd, and it was anyone's guess what they'd do to you. There were also rumors that Yeltsin supporters who had gathered in response to an appeal by Gaidar were preparing to march on the White House in an unarmed crowd. If even one shot were fired from the White House, it would be all the excuse the troops needed in order to calmly riddle the entire White House with bullets. This would also threaten to set off a massacre, since if anyone fired, you'd get a situation in which you'd never be able to work out what was happening.

(Tape-recorded testimony)

Yuriy Shikhov
FATHER NIKON — A PRIEST ON THE BARRICADES

Were many weapons handed out before the events of October 3?

I could see that all the defenders of the barricades were unarmed. Weapons were distributed only to soldiers and to fighters of the Russian National Unity, who I'm sure had all served in the army. However unpleasant Barkashov's theories might be, I have to say that his followers were disciplined people. They had iron discipline....

Where were you yourself while the shooting was going on?

At first I was in the room where I'd spent the night. This was the office of Yugin, the director of the parliamentary television station. Then I went down to Khasbulatov's reception room and met with the leaders of the parliament. There was a radio-telephone there. I informed the patriarchate four times about developments. I also appealed to the troops over the two-way radio.

What did you say to the troops?"

I said there were large numbers of women and children in the building, and asked the troops to stop shooting. They abused me, calling me "Father Gapon" [a police agent who was reputedly instrumental in setting up the "Bloody Sunday" massacre that helped spark the 1905 revolution]. It's true that their commanders rebuked them, telling them to watch their language. They said that everyone who was in the building should come out with a white flag, but they didn't explain where or how. If I was to lead people out, I had to know exactly where to go. I had to be sure we wouldn't be fired on, that all the snipers on the roofs had been warned.

The authorities' chief crime was that they launched an assault without presenting any conditions or giving any warnings, even though they knew how many people there were in the White House. They acted as if the people in the building were some gang of thugs. That's not to mention the fact that there was no analysis of the events at Ostankino—who was shooting at whom, who fired first, who was taking part in the attack.... Rutskoi on the balcony wasn't the entire Supreme Soviet, much less the entire Congress of People's Deputies. How can these bodies be held responsible for his statements? There was bloodshed at Ostankino, and that was terrible, intolerable, but why was it necessary to shed three times as much blood at the building of the Supreme Soviet?"

(*Segodnya,* October 28, 1993)

Anatoliy Nabatov, artist
MACHINE-GUNNED PEOPLE, MACHINE-GUNNED PICTURES

...In Yugin's office there was a priest. He knelt between the windows where a little iconostasis had been set up, and prayed. Yugin himself sat in a corner. There were other people in the room, all of them on the floor, including the first people who had been wounded. Someone shouted to the priest to stop, but Yugin said sternly, "Keep on praying, Father!" The priest was very pale, finding himself for the first time in the same mess as the rest of us. Bending down, and without rising from his knees, he prayed fervently. In the chamber of the parliament during the afternoon, he recited the burial service for those who had been killed.

We were already having to step over corpses as we walked. The barricades of furniture could not, of course, provide protection against bullets, but they could stop shell splinters, and they provided a strange feeling of security.

There still wasn't any shooting along the length of the corridors, and the most dangerous thing was to pass by the doorways....

Rutskoi had ordered people not to shoot back, and while the shooting was going on I remembered the words he'd said when I presented him with my picture:

"There's no idea worth shooting people for. It just can't exist in principle!"

You couldn't deny that he had consistency. In the light of all these events, his words seem particularly meaningful and symbolic.

The greatest danger wasn't from the tanks that were firing at concentrations of people in the White House, but from snipers. Many corridors were now under constant fire from them. When we went through into the hall of the Soviet of Nationalities, a man with an automatic rifle ran past, telling us as he went that he'd located a sniper. Running up to his commander, the fighter asked permission to shoot at this sniper. The commander didn't grant it. Later I discovered that my close friend Sasha Sidelnikov, a producer with the Lennauchfilm studio, had been killed in Devyatinskiy Lane. The friends who'd been with him later insisted that an expert study be conducted, and the experts confirmed that he'd been shot by a sniper. That's why the defenders of the White House were only trying to kill snipers. But any point from which they fired came under fire immediately from the tanks. Several times we tried to take out women, children, and wounded people.

....The corridors were now filled with corpses and with torn-off limbs. There was nowhere to take them. The Alpha group were in our midst. When they led us out onto the ramp in front of the White House, I was astonished to recognize the Alpha officer as a man who had been next to me in the chamber of the Soviet of Nationalities.

By my calculations, which are admittedly subjective, there were several hundred dead. They weren't taking any wounded out of the White House.... This was obvious to the defenders who were retreating from floor to floor. Inside the White House they were maintaining an active return fire.

(*Pravda,* December 21, 1993)

Ruslan Aushev: "I Tried to Save the Unarmed People...."
(Recorded by Vladimir Snegirev)

....Leaders who had gathered from throughout Russia were trying to work out what was happening. They were phoning about, heatedly discussing the situation around the White House.... At midday a report arrived that there were many casualties, and that women and even children remained inside the building of the former parliament. Of course, you couldn't remain indifferent in a situation like that. We decided to try to save people, those who were unarmed.... I suggested that we go to the Krasnopresnenskaya Embankment. I phoned Kolesnikov, the head of the General Staff, and Semenov, the Commander-in-Chief of the Land Forces, and asked for a temporary ceasefire. They agreed. We took two white flags, and at about 2 p.m. we went with Ilyumzhinov in a car, and drove right up to the main entrance to the White House. There was no firing from heavy weapons, but automatic fire was continuing.

We talked to a colonel of the Interior Ministry forces who was taking shelter from the bullets behind the ramp near entrance number twenty-four—this was the right-hand pediment of the building. Once again we asked him to moderate the attack for a while. But the shooting was going on in a disorderly fashion, from various points....

Raising the white flags, we went into the entrance. Inside on the ground floor, airborne troops were running around, firing into the openings of the stairways. We were taken up to the fifth floor. In a small room I saw Rutskoi and Achalov. Both were in camouflage dress, and Rutskoi was wearing running shoes. On the floor lay Rumyanstev, the secretary of the Constitutional Commission, trying to get in touch with someone by radiophone. Then Khasbulatov came in. I also saw Urazhtsev; as I remember, he was talking on a two-way radio. Khasbulatov was paler than usual, and Rutskoi looked agitated. From somewhere came a boy about eight years old.

I explained that we'd come to get the unarmed people out of the building. The reply was as follows: "We're all ready to lay down our arms. A ring of troops should be placed around the building and our safety should be guaranteed when we come out...." We were told that a large group of defenders had already tried to leave the building under a white flag, but that the gunfire had driven them all back.

(*Trud*, October 6, 1993)

4
AFTERMATH

On October 4, Moscow carried on with its normal life. The rolling thunder of heavy machine guns came from the center of town, intermingled from eleven o'clock on with the hollow boom of tank artillery, but at a distance of as little as 1.5 kilometers from the bullet-ridden House of Soviets, the streets were full of pedestrians as usual. All the shops were open, and urban public transportation was working. At Moscow State University, we continued with our work.

At Pushkin Square, Moscow residents hurried about their business. Entering and leaving the metro, they passed a large barricade on which various "defenders of democracy" had spent the night. Now, beneath the warm, bright rays of the morning sun, the people on the barricade struck picturesque poses for the photographers and television journalists who appeared from time to time. Meanwhile, near the next metro station, around the White House, other barricades were smashed apart by armored vehicles and abandoned by their surviving defenders. Those who had not left the barricades lay nearby in pools of blood.

The quiet in the city was deceptive. Moscow residents, whatever their views, were listening with acute anxiety to the artillery barrage reverberating from the city center. In the areas near the Krasnopresnenskaya Embankment, the crackle of machine-gun and rifle fire and the single sniper shots that cut into the rare minutes of silence made it impossible to forget the whirlwind of death blowing around the walls of the Russian parliament. About midday, a pillar of black smoke, rising from the House of Soviets, could be seen from all around.

The militia and other forces subject to the Interior Ministry did not ensure that the region surrounding the fighting was sealed off. Starting in the morning, crowds of curious onlookers began to gather around the House of Soviets. Most of these people flocked to the New Arbat (Kalinin Prospekt), to the bridge that crosses the Moscow River from the Hotel Ukraine to a point near the mayor's office, and to the embankment next to the Hotel Ukraine. At other places as well, large numbers of people stood and gaped. Dozens gathered on the roofs of nearby buildings.

The risk of being hit by a stray bullet was high, but the sightseers took no heed of this. People even crowded around the four tanks that were firing point-blank on the House of Soviets from the bridge; this was clearly visible from the Cable News Network coverage. After some time, these people were driven back with bursts of automatic rifle fire over their heads.

A good many Muscovites regarded what was happening as a free show. Others came to exult in the downfall of the Supreme Soviet. Still others mistrusted the official mass media, and decided to see for themselves what was happening.

Some of the onlookers paid for their curiosity with their lives.

Not all the spectators, however, remained passive. Around eleven or twelve o'clock, several thousand supporters of the Supreme Soviet, mainly young people, tried to break through to the besieged House of Soviets from the side of the Garden Ring Road. The troops set out to stop them, shooting to kill with automatic rifles, and the marchers halted and turned back. But later they flung themselves into the breach again.

Many people died in this despairing and hopeless attempt to reverse the course of events. But despite the mortal dangers, between noon and 1 p.m.

The woman at center was the last in a group of journalists to take cover when the corridors they were passing through came under fire from government snipers. She was wounded around 10 a.m. on October 4, and could not be treated until 5 p.m.

[Photo by Vojtech Lavicka]

some 150 to 200 people broke through to the main staircase of the House of Soviets, a development that was clearly visible on CNN. There they were met by airborne troops and by ranks of Interior Ministry soldiers equipped with shields, who forced them away from the entrance. Fortunately, the troops did not open fire on the unarmed demonstrators.

A few of these daring people even managed to get inside the House of Soviets, and to relay information to the defenders on what was happening outside.

Meanwhile, the battle continued. The situation was bizarre; three or four hundred people armed with light weapons were holding off an assault by some 1500 troops, including thoroughly trained special forces detachments, supported by fire from dozens of heavy machine guns, from automatic cannon, and from the artillery pieces of four tanks. Over the burning White House, now no longer white, two helicopters appeared, circled around, and flew off. Rumors then began to circulate around Moscow that the pilots had refused to open fire on the House of Soviets.

From the CNN coverage, it was clear that there was no organized defense of the building, that there was practically no answering fire, and that the defenders had no heavy weapons at their disposal. They managed to put out of action only two of the dozens of armored personnel carriers openly positioned around the House of Soviets. The sole armored personnel carrier that had been captured when the mayor's office had been stormed the previous day managed to fire only a few shots before it was put out of action by concentrated fire from the attackers. When its crew tried to abandon the machine, they were not taken prisoner. All of them were cut down by rifle and machine gun fire.

Toward five o'clock in the afternoon, the television began broadcasting reports that the defenders of the House of Soviets were capitulating. At first it was said that the Alpha group had captured the people who were leading the defense of the White House. Later it became clear that this was untrue, and that the defenders of the House of Soviets had surrendered of their own accord.

By evening the shooting had begun to die away. From our apartment building, the House of Soviets was clearly visible, our line of sight only partly blocked by other buildings. The white walls were half blackened, and were wrapped in clouds of smoke.

Dusk fell. In the darkness we could see tongues of flame in the windows of the House of Soviets. An apartment building nearby was also on fire. As was explained later, the upper floors of this building came under fire from machine guns and automatic cannon after a sniper was discovered on the roof.

Night descended on the city. The shooting had almost ceased in the area of the House of Soviets, but from time to time it flared up in other regions of the city. At one point a fierce burst of gunfire broke out around the New Arbat, scarcely less intense than during the assault on the White House. The sky was cut by tracer bullets, heavy machine guns and rifles clattered, and from time to time single shots were heard. After several minutes the shooting died away, but later it broke out again elsewhere....

Meanwhile, the House of Soviets remained on fire. The apartment building next to it continued to burn as well. The fire became even more intense; the red tongues of flame were clearly visible against the black night sky. The buildings were still burning at 8 p.m., at 10 p.m., and at midnight. They burned all night. Only toward morning were the firefighters, who had already arrived at the House of Soviets during the evening, allowed to put the fires out.

The fact that no immediate attempt was made to extinguish the blaze in the House of Soviets can be explained. Individual defenders refused to surrender, and there was a danger that shooting would break out. In places, the building was booby-trapped. But no arguments can justify the fact that the firefighters were not permitted to fight the blaze in the apartment block. An order was most likely issued to seal off the area of fighting and not to allow anyone through. And so, no one was allowed through.

The city sank into an uneasy sleep. For the first time since 1918, Moscow had seen the face of civil war. It was an ugly face—bloody and smoke-blackened, with the sour smell of burnt artillery powder.

Sebastian Job (Australia)
THE RUSSIAN WHITE HOUSE WON AND LOST

By eleven I have walked to the White House. Like the mayor's building, it is burning. The attack is not massive, but it is too much and more than enough. Defeat for the parliamentarians is inevitable. Nothing here is unexpected.

Except this. Down on the White House grounds, I mix with a couple of thousand people. They look like spectators, unarmed boys in their late teens. They act like protesters.

The OMON cannot hold them back. They surge out into the middle of the battle. More join them, forcing a halt to tanks and machine guns. I am amazed: they are reversing fate, setting civilian determination against guns, rescuing compromise from defeat.

So, Yeltsin's snipers begin to kill them. They run. And return. Again and again. More die. Young men, suddenly dead. Their bodies, and those of the dead, are rushed past me to ambulances waiting under the bridge. They are still being carried off when the surrender comes. I know their deaths will be written up in official histories as black and white as the burning building they fell for.

(Manuscript testimony)

Interview with Aleksandr Strakhov. Obtained by Andrei Kolganov

...In the morning, before the tanks began firing, there was a report on the two-way radio that a large crowd was moving toward Vosstanie

Square, and that at Vosstanie Square its path was being blocked by special forces troops. Over the radio we could hear incessant bursts of automatic rifle fire—there was no need to say more. Just like at the movies, you could hear continuous shooting.

...But before this we had time to look around. On the roof of the corner building, at the end of Kalinin Prospekt, there were huge numbers of people, and we could see that still more were climbing up. There was a huge crowd on the bridge. Large numbers of people were at the ramp where we came out. Their way was being blocked down below.

There was the impression that some kind of performance had been organized, and that people had come and taken their seats in the boxes and the dress circle, in order to get a good view.

(Tape-recorded testimony)

Eyewitness Testimonies. Recorded by Nadezhda Bondarenko

...Around ten or eleven o'clock on the morning of October 4, when the shooting had already begun, I was standing on the bridge near the mayor's office. Dead and wounded were being carried past me. As well as the citizens who were there out of conviction, there were also casual sightseers present. They were behaving in all sorts of ways. It wasn't just a matter of political convictions, people also have moral standards.... It's clear there were also provocateurs present, because several times I heard open appeals for people to engage in looting. Meanwhile, other people were helping the wounded or taking peaceful residents out of the zone that was under fire.... Personally I tried to persuade the people there to stop the bloodshed, but of course no one listened to me. I also began helping to carry away the wounded, and then when the stream of wounded diminished somewhat, I decided simply to go home.

A BEATING, MANDATE OR NO....
(Related by former people's deputy of the Supreme Soviet of the Russian Federation Yuriy Lodkin, who on October 4 went to the White House with a peacemaking mission, and was subsequently jailed. Recorded by Vasiliy Andreev)

...We saw on CNN what was happening at the White House....

Everyone became very agitated, saying "We've got to do something, we've got to stop this...." Without thinking particularly about the consequences, we made two white flags from the curtains of the Constitutional Court, and led by the President of the Ingush Republic, Ruslan Aushev, and by the President of Kalmykiya, Kirsan Ilyumzhinov, we set off in government cars for the House of Soviets.

We drove over from the Moskvoretskaya Embankment, went up the steps from the right-hand side, and with difficulty fought our way through the crowd to the White House. The crowd was uniformly hostile to the deputies. The enraged people paid no attention to the negotiators' flags, and tried to vent their anger on us. We made our way nearer. Then, with the major and the colonel who came out to meet us, we went another seventy meters or so, after which they told us: "Only Aushev and Ilyumzhinov will go into the White House, and you'll stay behind." We waited at a first aid station. The shooting didn't stop. Eight stretchers carrying wounded people were borne past us. There was blood, and people were groaning....

We waited for some time before Aushev and Ilyumzhinov reappeared. Once again, they made their way with difficulty through the furious crowd. I was amazed—"What kind of people are these, who are they protecting here, or who are they attacking?" There couldn't be any answer. Even Aushev and Ilyumzhinov had difficulty fighting their way free of the crowd and getting into one of our two cars.

With the Deputy Chairperson of the Council of Ministers of Mordovia, Fedor Tyurkin, I got into the car of the bodyguards of the President of Kalmykiya....

We hadn't managed to go more than a few meters when people armed to the teeth leapt on us. They pulled us out of the car, shouting, "Lie down on the ground, you sons of bitches!" No one listened to our explanations about our peacemaking mission. Or more precisely, they didn't want to listen. "Get your face on the asphalt, hands by your sides!" They kicked our stretched-out arms with their steel-capped boots, then stamped with their heels on our heads and on our kidneys.... I was probably lucky. I managed to move my hat, which had fallen from my head, under my face, and the felt cushioned my head from the kicks with steel-capped boots. There was nothing to protect my back. Pain, anger, and humiliation.... But if you said a word, you immediately received a kick in the kidneys. They beat us with professional thoroughness.... Then the command, "Get up!", and they made us run the gauntlet. Earlier, I'd imagined that such a thing was possible only in films about the tsarist era.... Now I discovered for myself what it meant to run the gauntlet.

There were seven of us, and every armed OMON member considered it his duty to hit every one of us with the muzzle or butt of his rifle, or to kick us. We were made to run for five hundred meters....

"Lieutenant, let me have this one, I'll carve him up!" Perhaps it was luck, or perhaps the general confusion that stopped them, but the seven of us were not carved up.

Who were these people? I now know that they were the heroic Vityaz group. The lieutenant from Ilyumzhinov's guard had a standard pistol, provided to him in connection with his duties. When they found it, they beat him appallingly. The man bore all this steadfastly, but whether his health will stand it, I don't know. Then they crammed twenty-five of us into a van and took us to 38 Petrovka Street—that symbol of the struggle against lawbreakers.

They took us there, and beat us again. After that they got a new group of detainees, just ordinary people in most cases. People in camouflage dress flung themselves on these new arrivals with an animalistic fury. They beat them so ferociously that the militia major on duty, who had apparently seen everything through the window, couldn't stand it anymore. He ran out into the yard, and in an inhuman-sounding voice started shouting: "Stop it! What are you doing? Stop it!" They stopped.

....Then Yura Kozlov, an ambulance driver from Golyanov, was put in our cell. The people in camouflage dress had grabbed him at the White House when he and a friend had come to look at the "revolution." The valiant Vityaz bashed him so hard that they broke several of his ribs.... They also beat Deputy Chairperson of the Council of Ministers of Mordovia Tyurkin so hard that on the third day I could still see terrible bruises on his back.

(*Pravda,* November 3, 1993)

The tragic conflict in Moscow did not end with the surrender by the defenders of the House of Soviets. Although armed resistance by Yeltsin's opponents ceased, many important developments still lay ahead. These were to have a profound effect on Russia's political climate and on the moral state of Russian society. The victors, it appeared, set out to use every possible means to undermine their earlier authority in the eyes of society.

VICTORS AND VANQUISHED

About 1500 noncombatants left the House of Soviets. They included deputies, members of the staff of the Supreme Soviet, service personnel, and people who were simply supporters of the parliament. In addition, no fewer than 300 volunteers had fought with arms in hand, and a considerable number of people had joined the special regiment formed to defend the parliament, but had not received weapons. The first small group, which contained a considerable number of deputies, was put in buses and taken off some distance from the House of Soviets. The buses then departed, but the group remained encircled by the crowd of Yeltsin supporters, and its members were subjected to insults and blows.

Most of the people who were evacuated from the House of Soviets were less fortunate. Those who were suspected of having put up armed resistance were sent to the nearby Krasnaya Presnya stadium, where a filtration point was set up. All that night and all the following morning, residents in nearby apartment buildings heard bursts of automatic gunfire coming from the direction of the stadium. Filtration was under way.

A thousand or more noncombatants waited by the main staircase of the House of Soviets for the promised buses to arrive, but the buses failed to come. Before long it grew dark. Suddenly a massive fusillade broke out, aimed at the House of Soviets. People fled along the Krasnopresnenskaya Embankment in the opposite direction from the shooting, heading away from the mayor's office. They ran through the courtyards of the apartment buildings.

There, beneath unlit archways, the OMON were waiting for them. The fortunate people were the ones who were only subjected to searches accompanied by blows from rifle butts, fists, and heavy boots, and who lost their money and valuables. Some were viciously beaten. Others—who failed to stop on demand, tried to protest, displayed resistance, or were simply chance victims of bursts of automatic fire unleashed on some random impulse—remained lying in these courtyards.

The night of October 4 and 5 will remain forever in the memory of those who survived it.

During October 4 and 5, the people who counted themselves on the side of the victors revealed their proclivities in all their splendor. On the afternoon of October 4, looting had already broken out in the vicinity of the White House. Of cars that had been left near the building, no more than the empty shells remained. From trucks and from containers standing on them, everything that could possibly be carried off was taken. The looting continued even as bullets flew. On October 5, the less courageous hauled away whatever had survived the raids by those whom the shooting had been unable to deter. What the bullets did not destroy, the bandits pillaged. Some of the looters were arrested, but this did not alter the general picture.

After this, the victors began to reinforce their claims to power by imposing a curfew and by outlawing opposition parties and organizations, without court orders or even any reference to the law. Unsympathetic press organs were also banned in just as illegal a manner. During the curfew, in more than a few cases, law enforcement patrols helped themselves without payment to goods from commercial kiosks, extracted bribes from curfew breakers, and opened fire at any shadow they imagined they saw in a dark alleyway.

Using the excuse provided by the curfew, Moscow Mayor Luzhkov instigated a campaign of ethnic cleansing in the city. The militia and OMON began to arrest people who lacked a Moscow residence permit and to throw them out of the Russian capital, despite the fact that the "democrats" had earlier made fiery denunciations of the residence permit system. The main people to suffer from the mayor's new policy were petty traders from the Caucasus and Central Asia, and also the numerous refugees. To these people, the militia and OMON continued applying the tactics they had already found so advantageous for dealing with unarmed civilians: taunts, beatings, thefts, and bribes.

References to the struggle against organized crime were hypocritical. While the struggle was being waged against the "Caucasian mafia" (or more precisely, against the people from whom the Caucasian mafia levied tribute), the Moscow mafia planned—and after the repeal of the state of emergency, successfully executed—a series of hired killings of business entrepreneurs. Among the victims was the director of Rosselkhozbank, the country's second-largest commercial bank.

Across the country rolled a wave of closures of opposition newspapers, and of firings of "unreliable" state employees. Despite his Decree No. 1400, Yeltsin suggested that the local organs of representative power should dissolve themselves, and that he himself would abolish those that refused to follow this advice. Under pressure from Yeltsin, the Constitutional Court ceased to function. The country prepared for free and democratic elections.

Story of an Eyewitness (Recorded by Nadezhda Bondarenko)
....Several people I didn't know went with me, young men and a young woman. We went through the courtyards, and ran into a group of armed people in black masks. At first I thought these were the notorious fighters. They ordered us to put our hands behind our heads, and led us off into a laneway, behind some trucks that were standing there. Other people in military uniform stood alongside these trucks. There I heard the following dialogue, which referred to me:

"And what'll we do with this one?"

"Thump him one and let him go."

After that they started beating me. The people in uniform didn't just "thump me one"; they beat me persistently over a long period. I fell down; they kicked me. They lifted me up by the collar, and beat me again.... I stood up again, and tried to get away, since I'd heard them being told to let me go.... But they caught me, and with the words "Where do you think you're going?" started beating me again. Then, when I couldn't stand up any more, and was only half conscious, they threw me into a bus. They threw a lot of people in there besides me. They were throwing people in there roughly and carelessly; people were lying on top of me, and the weight of their bodies was crushing me, but I couldn't move. It was lucky for me that I was on the bottom, because the people on top were still getting beaten while the bus was driving along....

They took us to a militia station somewhere—I can't say exactly which one. They threw me and another man, who was completely unconscious, onto the asphalt next to the station entrance. We lay there for a long time. Finally, someone remembered us. To see if we were alive, they stubbed cigarettes on us. The man lying next to me had his ear burnt with a cigarette, because he stubbornly refused to show any signs of life. Then it turned out that he was alive after all, though he had internal injuries. When they jabbed a cigarette into my face, I opened my eyes and saw in front of me a man in uniform with an automatic rifle slung around his neck. Looking at me, he said in an indifferent sort of way, "Maybe we should shoot him and throw him out?" I found the strength to raise myself up a little and reply: "Either shoot me, or take me into the station and don't torture me, because I've already been lying for two hours on bare asphalt." They took me by the legs and dragged me into the station. Dragged me like a corpse, banging my head on every step.... Then when an ambulance eventually came, they tried to drag me out of the station to the vehicle in the same way. But the medics wouldn't have it, and forced the Interior Ministry people to take me out in the proper way, carrying me by the arms and legs.

In the hospital they told me that without medical attention I would have been dead within an hour and a half. They took out my spleen. What's going to happen to me now, I don't know. A representative of the prosecutor's office came to me in the hospital and demanded my signature on a document stating that I had no claims on the organs of the Interior Ministry. And I had to sign it, because I wanted to stay alive. In exchange, they promised not to touch me any more. And it's true, they didn't touch me as long as I was in the hospital, but then when I signed myself out and went home, the organs went back on their word.... Now they're calling me into the prosecutor's office for some reason, and if I don't turn up they're threatening to lay some kind of criminal charge on me. If I was sure that they really were going to charge me with something, and that I could hire a lawyer and defend myself, then I'd turn up. But I've already realized that there aren't any laws in Russia any more, and that I could simply disappear without trace. I haven't committed any crime, there's nothing to charge me with, but they don't want live witnesses. That's why I've gone into hiding.

But I've decided that if there's any harassment of the people who are publicizing my case, if the "democrats" try to accuse them of slander, I'll go to court anyway, and tell the truth no matter what it costs me.

Interview with Aleksandr Strakhov. Obtained by Andrei Kolganov

We went around gathering people, and then we all went out together. We'd already taken the first group out and sent them off in the buses.

With the second group there were deputies as well. We went out through the central entrance, and they told us to go one at a time. I went first, and with me went the same young man and woman, and we came out by the central staircase. They stopped us on the bottom steps. The Alpha detachment was there; they told us that buses were coming, and that we'd be taken on these buses to the nearest metro. This lasted a long time. We thanked the airborne troops, who had formed up in a corridor, thanked them for turning around their cannon and not firing, and for taking action to stop the shooting. I hadn't heard this second hand—I'd seen it myself.

We stopped on the bottom steps, and there they let out quite a large number of journalists, including some with photographic equipment and video cameras. Directly opposite, on the other side of the embankment, was a huge crowd, a real sea of people. There were tanks there as well. There were still more people on the roofs of the buildings. We were reminded of our earlier impression that someone had organized a sort of theater, with boxes and balconies.

I forgot to mention another episode. When we came out to hold talks, they suddenly started shooting from the bridge on the huge number of people that were there. The people threw themselves to the ground, stood up, and ran. Then there was more shooting.... This was on the bridge. It was somewhere around 4:30 when they began firing on this crowd. I still don't know whose supporters they were.

Who was doing the shooting?

The troops, as I understand it. They were firing from the bridge. It was always very simple to work out where the shooting was coming from. They were shooting from the point directly opposite the one toward which people were running. We could hear this and see it—it was quite plain.

For a long time we waited on the bottom steps of the central staircase for the promised buses that were to take us away. We stood there for somewhere between forty minutes and an hour. No one was arrested, neither deputies nor ordinary civilians. I went up to the Alpha commanders and asked that we be taken away in the PAZ buses in which the detachment had obviously come—there were six or seven of them standing there. The commanders refused to do this, saying that these were the Alpha's buses, and that no one would be taken anywhere in them. Other buses were coming, and we'd be taken away in those.

The light was beginning to fade, the sun was setting, and in fifteen or twenty minutes it would be dark. The day had been very sunny—we could see this inside in the dark corridor from the fact that the sunlight was coming under the doors. Suddenly the shooting started up again. People rushed down the sides of this staircase, and behind the low granite walls at the sides, in order to take shelter. The shooting was again coming from the direction of the humpbacked bridge. Continuous firing had begun again.

While we were standing there, we looked at the building. The clock had stopped at three minutes past ten. Four floors, from the top down, were on fire. Because the wind was blowing from the right, the flames were constantly spreading from one room to the next on these floors. Panes of glass were falling from the windows. It was clear that an inferno was raging, and that the wind was blowing it further and further. At this moment, fifteen minutes after sunset, darkness descended rapidly. In view of everything that had happened up to that point, it would have been absurd to have hoped that they wouldn't fire, or that they wouldn't take aim because of the darkness. People rushed along the embankment to the left, supposing one were facing toward the central entrance—that is, they rushed in the direction of the International Trade Center.

At the first building to the left of the House of Soviets, either the OMON or the airborne troops let us through into the courtyard by way of a shop window and the shop itself. Disorderly shooting was going on there, and it was there that the deputy Baburin was arrested. I stress this because no one was arrested while we were on the staircase, neither deputies, nor ordinary civilians, no one. And Baburin was arrested there in the courtyard. They screamed out, "Hands behind your head!" fired a burst over his head, and grabbed him. There were a lot of people, and they began to scatter....

A lot—how many was that approximately?

Hundreds, at least 300, that's certain. Also, this man who had described himself as a representative of the ZiL trade union had gone off arm in arm with three women toward this very building long before this, when everyone was standing on the staircase. Earlier, he'd been running up and down continuously with a loudspeaker, saying that that the buses would be there any minute, but then he himself headed off separately with three women.

In the courtyard, people scattered into the entrances to the building, and we ran into one of them as well. I still had this young man and woman with me. I was literally arm in arm with them; I told the woman that I didn't want her mother to lose her at the age of sixteen. I'd given her a helmet taken from someone who'd been killed; she'd gone to the talks in this helmet, and she was wearing it in the courtyard as well. We sat for a considerable time in a stairwell. At first we tried asking to be let into apartments. No one in a single apartment opened their door to us. Naturally, no one wanted to go into the courtyards, where they were shooting without warning. A few people climbed up into the attic, and said there were snipers sitting there; that is, they saw armed people in the attic. After this we sat in the stairwell on the lower floors, intending to wait until everything was over.

After approximately an hour, groups of four, five, or six people started leaving the building entrance, hoping to find some way of breaking through. In my group there were six people. Once again I had the two young people with me. There was another man, and an elderly couple of about sixty-five, very intelligent-looking people. They had a basket; obviously, they'd brought something with them. The man was limping badly, and when we leapt out of the entrance, it was clear that we'd have to head off by various routes. We saw where the previous group had gone. We went along the wall of the building to an archway, and from one archway to another, leading onto a street running parallel to the embankment. There we ran into armed airborne troops, and there was shooting. We hid behind some columns. Behind these same columns we found the corpse of a man, lying in a pool of blood.

The young woman became very scared. At first she couldn't understand—she was saying, "Who's this, why's he lying there?... What, is he dead?" The old people told us to break through on our own. They were saying, "We're old folk, it'll probably be easier for us to get out, they won't shoot at us." As it later turned out, this wasn't true. We went through another archway, making our way through the courtyards. At a particular moment we came out from behind the corner of one of the buildings onto an open space. There at a building entrance was a very bright light. There was a shout: "Stop, or we'll shoot!" We shouted back that they shouldn't shoot, that we were civilians, that we weren't armed, and leapt into the nearest entrance. We climbed up, and at first sat on the staircase. We realized that there would be round-ups, and seeing what was going on in the courtyards, we understood that staying where we were was senseless. We had to think of something that would allow us to go further and break through. We tried asking at apartment doors, hoping that someone would at least let the young woman in, but no one would admit even her; not a single door was opened. She stood in front of the peephole, saying, "I'm sixteen years old, I'm scared, they're shooting and killing people on the streets, I won't even come into the rooms, I'll sit in the hallway." Not a single door was opened....

It's true that after long discussions someone gave us a drink—they brought out a jar full of water. An hour or two later, we managed to persuade the man living in this apartment to come out with us and his dog, and with his documents showing that he was a local resident. We went out into the courtyard. Once again the shout: "Stop or I'll shoot! You with the dog—stay where you are! The first in line come here!" I went first. They forced me up against the wall with my legs apart and searched me, and then did the same with the others. After this we asked to be allowed to proceed to the metro, explaining that we'd been there in the stairwell, saying that there was shooting going on round about, and asking them to take us through.

On the street parallel to the embankment stood dozens of armored personnel carriers, and a large number of soldiers. It was now around 11 p.m. We chose the following tactic: we asked to have one soldier take us to the next post, because we were scared. I'm not ashamed to admit it—I was really scared, because I'd seen corpses, seen that there was shooting going on in the courtyards, and I had no wish whatsoever to be hit by those bullets. We chose the tactic of going out deliberately into illuminated areas so that the troops could see who was coming. I went in front with the young woman, so that it was clear that we were coming openly, that we were civilians, and that we were unarmed. In the end, we managed to get through the large number of posts, many of which were in the darkest back streets, next to large numbers of armored personnel carriers. Soon after eleven we came out at the Ulitsa 1905 Goda metro station. The streets there were dead. There were virtually no people around—no more than a handful. Finding this station closed, we literally ran to the Begovaya metro station, and arrived there around 11:30.

(Tape-recorded testimony)

WE ASPIRED TO COMMUNISM, BUT FINISHED UP IN RUSSIA
Excerpts from the book by Stanislav Govorukhin, *The Great Criminal Revolution*
Eyewitness Testimony by Oleg Germanovich Rumyantsev

....We stood for a long time at the main entrance, underneath the coat of arms. There were two small buses there, but we weren't put in them. While keeping an eye on us, the members of the Alpha group explained something. One of the officers said, "It's too bad, I'd rather they were taken away."

The command rang out: "Forward!" We set off to the right, toward the nearest building.

Now I know why they needed the legend about snipers from the White House. To justify the meat grinder they had set up in the courtyards and entranceways.

We walked up to the building, and the Alpha group lagged behind us. An OMON member, or perhaps one of the militia, leapt out of the entrance with an automatic rifle. He screamed out, "Lie down, you sons of bitches!" They pushed me into the entrance. A drunk man seized me by the beard: "Come here, you with the kike face!" Three times he hit me in the face with his knee. Then they went through my pockets; they didn't find any money, but they took a small Sony radio. Several times they hit me on the torso, around the kidneys. The entranceway was a through passage, and they forced me toward the exit. An officer (I think he was an officer) whispered to me: "They're shooting in the courtyard. Run to that entrance!" We ran to the entrance he had indicated....

We ran inside. There we found the same thing, the same hell, only a different circle. The OMON were beating two young men, who for some reason had been stripped to the waist. They were mere adolescents, no more than about seventeen—defenders of the White House. The OMON hit one of them in the ribs with a rifle, so hard that the cracking of bones was audible.

They grabbed me and hit me several times in the testicles.

After that I was passing blood in my urine for a week. It was at this time that Pochinok declared to the press that I had applied to him for material aid.... [Pochinok was a former People's Deputy of the Russian Federation who quit his post when Yeltsin announced various material and official privileges for those who repudiated the Supreme Soviet. He was given the post of Deputy Minister of Finance, and was appointed to head the commission in charge of finding jobs for and paying compensation to those former deputies who were judged sufficiently loyal to the regime].

They forced us out into the courtyard with their rifle butts. There really was shooting there. It was unclear who they were shooting at, but we could hear single shots....

An OMON member rose up before me. He worked the bolt of his rifle. Imagine the situation: a drunk man with an automatic rifle, his eyes totally inhuman, and at his feet, only a little to one side, someone's corpse. "Right, you son of a bitch, kiss your life goodbye!" he said, coming up to me. Twice he spat in my face, and then screamed, "Turn around!" I turned my back to him. "On your knees!" And he let fly with a burst over my head.

I lay there, without the strength to get up. Out of the corner of my eye I saw deputy Shashviashvili come out of the doorway I had just come through; the OMON knocked him from his feet and began kicking him with their boots. Deputy Fakhrutdinov came out. He looked as though he were just coming from a sitting—in a tie, with his briefcase. The OMON ran up to him. Fakhrutdinov announced self-importantly: "I'm a deputy from the independent republic of Tatarstan!" "Dirty wog Tatar!" And using all their strength, they began hitting him on the head with their rifle-butts. Fakhrutdinov is now in the hospital in critical condition.

While they were beating Fakhrutdinov, I stood up and ran, no longer caring what happened. I ran into an entranceway and began pressing all the doorbells one after another. No one opened a door. There were people in the apartments; I could hear the barking of dogs, but no one let me in....

"Let me in!" I begged. "I'm deputy Rumyantsev, they're shooting at us!"

"Get fucked!" "Serve you right!" "I've got children...."

I ran into another entrance. There on the steps sat Sazhi Umalatova, the beaten Shashviashvili, deputy Saenko, and an elderly woman. A young man with a shaved head and running shoes came in. He smelled of vodka and blood. He took a look at us and left.

"That's their scout!"

"Let's get out of here."

We split up. I went with an elderly woman, taking her by the arm....

Suddenly, out in the middle of the courtyard, I saw a gang of men. Like the scout, they had shaved heads and running shoes....

I sensed the physical presence of death. A voice rang out from the darkness. "Stop! Come here, you bastards!" A peal of laughter, and again a voice: "Come here!"

We didn't stop to talk, but flung ourselves into the bushes. A shot rang out. We rushed into an entrance, ran up to the second floor, and rang the first doorbell. The door opened immediately. Behind it was a woman. "I'm deputy Rumyantsev." "We know you. Come in."

It was a one-room apartment, inhabited by a family of three people. I stayed there several days....

(*Novaya Yezhednevnaya Gazeta,* November 12, 1993)

Anatoliy Nabatov, artist
MACHINE-GUNNED PEOPLE, MACHINE-GUNNED PAINTINGS
Testimony of an eyewitness

It's a complete lie that the people leaving the White House were provided with buses. It's true that when I came out of the building, people said there had been two buses. They took some people off to drink coffee, and others to Lefortovo Prison. The rest of us, about 1500 people, gathered on the ramp in front of the ambassadors' entrance. We stood there for a long time. The Alpha group checked us over for weapons, and protected us from the militia, who kept trying to taunt us.

After a period of quiet, the shooting started up again. The troops started by methodically shooting into the top floors. Then their aim moved lower and lower, until they were pouring bullets into the ground floor. Then the Alpha group took responsibility for leading the whole crowd off to the residential buildings next to the White House. The Alpha group itself didn't know what was happening. They had been promised buses, and they promised us buses in turn. Then they realized that they themselves had been set up. They took us to the apartment buildings and left us to our fate. But the nightmare continued there.

The whole crowd, in small groups or individually, began moving off toward the Ulitsa 1905 Goda metro station. We didn't know it then, but the station was closed. Ahead of us, meanwhile, were numerous patrols of blind-drunk OMON members, convinced we were all "commies."

At first we heard isolated shots and bursts of gunfire; then they became more and more frequent. There would be a shot; then a scream; then silence. The OMON were shooting even at shadows. We made our way along walls and through bushes. I stood with a group next to a wall and listened. Here I recognized Yuriy Mikhailovich Voronin, Khasbulatov's deputy. I was astonished to find they'd let him go. Here also were Lidiya Shipovalova and a number of other deputies. Further on, someone was being beaten. A woman ran past, screaming: "They're killing all the young ones!" The shots were coming closer and closer. I tried to get into an entranceway, but it was locked. Then another, and thank God, it was open. Shots followed me.

Unfortunately, I can't give the name of the people who saved me. What would be the point of exposing them to reprisals? It's remarkable that there were still people who opened their doors at a time like that. There were already six people like me in this apartment.

(*Pravda*, December 21, 1993)

Boris Glebov
A HOMELESS MAN WITH A KREMLIN PASS

On October 16 the doorbell rang in the apartment where Vladimir Klebanov was living. His question "Who's there?" brought the classic reply: "Open up, there's a telegram for you."

Klebanov thought another invitation had arrived from President Yeltsin to attend a sitting of the Constitutional Assembly. Yeltsin's last telegram to Klebanov had arrived on September 23.

But this was not an invitation to the Kremlin. Three cadets of the Orlovskiy Higher Academy of the Interior Ministry, armed with automatic rifles and equipped with helmets and bulletproof vests, burst into the apartment. They were accompanied by two officers of the militia, Captain Mikhail Dubinin and Lieutenant Vyacheslav Kudinov.

[Biographical note: Vladimir Aleksandrovich Klebanov was the organizer of the first independent union of miners in the USSR, established in the Donbass during the 1960s. The union was forcibly dissolved in September 1968, immediately after Klebanov's arrest and conviction.... Klebanov served about twenty years in all. Among others, Margaret Thatcher, Ronald Reagan, Francois Mitterand, and AFL-CIO president Kirkland called for his release. In the West, Klebanov was described as the Russian Walesa.]

After being released from prison in 1987 and undergoing rehabilitation, Klebanov returned to what he knew best—organizing an independent labor union which now counts no fewer than 130,000 members. In June 1993 Klebanov was invited to take part in the Constitutional Assembly.

The Interior Ministry employees who burst in on Klebanov on October 16 took the trade union leader not to the Kremlin, but to the 58th Militia Station. Here they finally explained to him the reason for his arrest. He had been detained for living illegally in Moscow, a charge punishable by deportation to his usual place of residence.

This was a harsh punishment, especially if one considers that Klebanov has no permanent place of residence. He was born in Borisov, Belarus; he was convicted in Donetsk, Ukraine; and he was released from custody in Tashkent, Uzbekistan. Accordingly, his passport does not contain a permit allowing him to live permanently in any city or town.

....When Klebanov pointed out to the militia officers that he was a member of the Constitutional Assembly, showing them his membership document (no. 0649) and his Kremlin pass, they told him that his document was invalid; by decree of President Yeltsin, all laws in Russia had been suspended, the Constitutional Assembly had been abolished under Decree No. 1400, and the deputies of the parliament had been dispersed—"They were all Yids." "You're one of the same lot—you all ought to be deported to Tel Aviv."

After this they started beating Klebanov viciously. When they had beaten him up, the militia officers threw him into a cell where there were already no fewer than twenty people, and where it was impossible even to sit down.

On the night of October 16, a reinforced squad of guards, armed with automatic rifles, took Klebanov to the Babushkinskiy sobering-up station. In this treatment facility for alcoholics, one of the blocks had been turned over completely to the detention of people arrested during the State of Emergency in Moscow.

In the sobering-up station, the militia photographed Klebanov in profile and full face. Then they began taking him around the Moscow "special distributors," trying, as they explained, to fix him up for a long time to come. But then they brought him back to the Babushkinskiy sobering-up station. They placed him in a cell where they had put anyone whose appearance suggested they might be of Caucasian nationality. The cell contained citizens even of Afghanistan and India, arrested evidently for the color of their skin.

Klebanov's ordeal came to an end when staff members of the sobering-up station released him from the institution. This was at 9 p.m. on October 17. Before setting him free, they hinted to him that the parting would not be for long, and that he should keep in mind the prison cell that for a long time had been yearning to have him back....

(*Obshchaya Gazeta*, October 29–November 4, 1993)

Yuriy Borisov, film director
FRAMES FROM THE PUTSCH

The corner of Rochdelskaya and Nikolayev streets. In a public telephone booth I counted eleven bullet holes. The bullets had been precisely aimed. One of them had passed through the telephone itself, just below the dialing apparatus. I deliberately calculated where the holes would have been in my own body. Yesterday when I was at this spot, preparing to call the editorial office, I'd managed by some miracle to throw myself down on the asphalt just before the booth above me was fired on from an armored personnel carrier. The cement rendering on the corner building had ended up like a sieve. All I saw at the time was the asphalt. All I heard was the gunfire and my own voice pulsating in my temples, "Our Father...."

The first-floor shops had been pillaged as thoroughly as if a Tatar horde had passed through. The manager of an Italian fashion salon, a plump, unshaven Georgian, related with a melancholy sigh that the previous day, as soon as the first shots rang out, a crowd of spectators had rushed up against the store windows, and, pushing out the bulletproof glass, had crammed themselves into the shop. When the last of them left, all that remained were the 1.5-meter stereo speakers.... Everything else had been taken, even an already-opened packet of powdered soap from the bathroom. It was sad to behold the devastation of a store that had been set up lovingly and with taste....

...Directly in front of me, a large trailer from a long-haul truck was blocking the road from a parapet on one side to a lawn on the other. The doors of the trailer had been flung open. Three young men had jumped inside, and were throwing down small and apparently light boxes at a furious pace, as though in a speeded-up film. Down below was a crowd of young people, eighty or a hundred of them; each grabbed two or three of the boxes and ran off just as quickly, literally within seconds. I realized they were looting, hesitating only when there was an unexpected burst of gunfire. The troops, charging into the crowd, grabbed about ten looters and stood them with their faces to the side of the same truck....

...I pushed my way through to the commander. After CNN had recorded him, he deigned to give an interview to the less prestigious print media. Senior Lieutenant A.K. Shepunov from the Vladimir OMON. A strong young man, confident of his own worth, with steely eyes and a firm, improbably clean-shaven chin. He explained:

"This group was probably organized beforehand. They hoped for big profits, but the container is full of crackers. Yesterday they cleaned out this side here"—shifting his cut-off Kalashnikov to his left hand, he pointed with his finger at the corrugated forty-foot container with the inscription CHOYNC—"and there they really found something worth carting off. Photocopiers, faxes, telephones.... By the time it was reported, and we'd got here ... half the stuff had already gone. And what was most interesting was they were under fire. A lot of people took part in the looting. Most of them were homeless and young people below draft age."

(*Solidarnost*, no. 23, 1993)

VICTIMS

Prior to the bloody events of October 3 and 4, there had been very few deaths on either side in the conflict. On the night of September 23 and 24 two people had died in obscure circumstances; it was unclear who was responsible. An officer of the militia had also died as a result of careless acts by his own colleagues on September 28. Rumors that people had died in the clashes on Smolenskaya Square on October 2 were not confirmed.

Were people killed during the clashes between demonstrators and the militia on October 3? Probably yes, though the precise number on each side is unknown, since the published data do not distinguish between the general death toll and those killed during the demonstration. Moreover, the data were reported on the basis of official categories—there are separate figures for the number of militia members killed, for deaths among the Interior Ministry troops and so forth—but this information relates to various periods. We know that one militia member apparently received fatal injuries when he fell between two maneuvering trucks of the militia or Interior Ministry forces. Several demonstrators also fell beneath these trucks. One of them lost his legs. The number of injured on both sides was considerable, running into the dozens. One demonstrator who was present when the blockade on the House of Soviets was broken died several hours later as a result of blows he received. Several demonstrators received gunshot wounds when snipers fired on them from the direction of the mayor's office.

Accounts of casualties during the storming of the mayor's office contradict each other. Both sides reported that people from their ranks were killed. To judge from these reports, the number of dead on each side could hardly have been more than four to six people.

Most of the casualties on October 3 resulted from the events at the Ostankino television center. Two of the defenders of the television center died, a soldier of the Vityaz special forces detachment and a television engineer. The number of dead among the demonstrators and the fighters of the armed group headed by General Makashov is unknown. Only the overall number of dead who were brought to Moscow morgues and hospitals on October 3 in known; this was sixty-six people. Since the number of people who died in other clashes during the afternoon and evening of October 3 was not more than ten or fifteen, the number killed at Ostankino can be put fairly confidently at around fifty. In addition, more than fifty people received serious gunshot wounds.

The overwhelming majority of those who were killed at Ostankino were unarmed demonstrators caught in crossfire from automatic rifles and heavy machine guns. There can be no talk in this case of a preplanned assault carried out by trained groups organized along military lines. The numbers

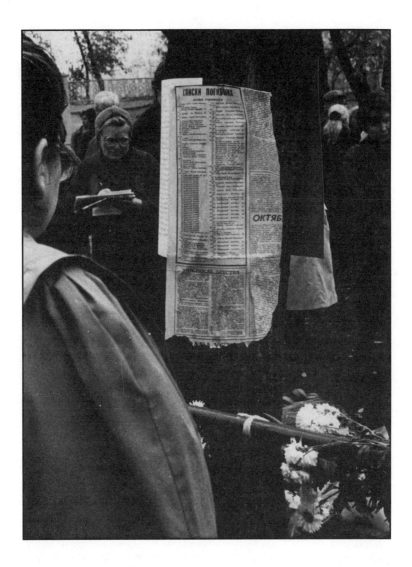

Several days after the attack on the White House, a newspaper compiled a list of names of the wounded and dead, using information gathered from city morgues and hospitals. Here, a woman copies the list. Flowers from a makeshift shrine for the victims lie nearby.

[Photo by Vojtech Lavicka]

of dead and wounded are witness to this. In a military operation, the number of wounded normally exceeds the number of dead several times over, but here the numbers were approximately equal. What occurred at Ostankino was the cold-blooded slaughter of people who had no chance to resist, or even to put up passive resistance. This is the reason for the unusually large number of dead in the overall casualty list.

On the morning of October 4, a considerable number of people, almost all unarmed, were shot down on the barricades around the House of Soviets and on Free Russia Square. Correspondents who managed to gain access to the House of Soviets immediately after the assault put the number of corpses around the building at anywhere from twenty to thirty people, most of them near the humpbacked bridge, where the defenders of the building had their main barricade.

There is no reliable information on the number of people killed inside the House of Soviets. If the total number of dead, including those who perished around the House of Soviets, is put at a little over 130 (as in the first official figure published by the medical examiner), when the official figure on the number of dead inside the House of Soviets—42 people—is added, one gets 172. The official overall figure for some reason rose only to 143 people. It seems we are entitled to believe the semi-official accounts according to which no one took particular trouble to calculate the number of people killed in the House of Soviets or to establish their identity. Unidentified corpses were taken to the morgues and were mixed there with corpses which had been brought in earlier from other places, mainly Ostankino.

A number of people were killed in the crowd that gathered to watch the assault on the White House. Most were killed by stray bullets or shell fragments from the heavy fire directed at the building by the attackers. Some were killed by sniper fire. To judge from their radio conversations, the attacking forces killed three or four snipers who might have been counted among the defenders of the Supreme Soviet. These snipers were aiming their fire at the attackers. At the same time, a large number of snipers who were aiming their fire at House of Soviets took up positions around the building. Some eyewitnesses say that these snipers often fired at any target that came within their telescopic sights, including the crowd of spectators and even their own forces.

A considerable number of people were killed following the surrender of the House of Soviets. These were the chance victims of the gunfire the militia, the OMON, and the Interior Ministry troops unleashed in the evening darkness, victims of shootings by victors drunk with vodka and arbitrary power. As a rule, those who were shot were people who tried to resist being beaten, or who looked too much like fighters who might have taken part in the armed defense of the House of Soviets. A large number of people were savagely beaten on their way from the House of Soviets or in militia stations.

If we are to believe the official reports on the number of dead, then a total of 77 people were killed on October 4 and subsequently. From the official total of 143 dead, we subtract 66 people who were killed on October 3 and during the night of October 3 and 4. From this figure of 77 people, we further subtract 28 armed forces and Interior Ministry personnel whom official data reported killed ... and further arithmetical exercises become pointless. The overall figure for the number killed includes only a part of the armed forces and Interior Ministry dead—those who were taken to Moscow morgues and hospitals. Consequently, any further calculations are necessarily imprecise. A number of sources give the figure 66 not just as the total of those who were killed on October 3, but also as the number who died during the assault on the House of Soviets on October 4. According to the newspaper *Segodnya* on October 7, a total of 66 corpses were taken to the morgues and hospitals during the afternoon of October 4; most of these people were probably onlookers outside the ring of attacking troops.

By May 1994, the official total was 162 dead. This included those who had died after being wounded

There is no way the figure of 77 killed on October 4 can include both the 43 dead (by official figures) inside the House of Soviets and the people killed on the barricades around the House of Soviets prior to the assault. The latter could not have been included in the figure of 66 dead delivered to the morgues and hospitals, since on the afternoon of October 4 they were still lying outside the House of Soviets. Moreover, the overall list included 29 people who, according to *Nezavisimaya Gazeta* on October 7, were officially recorded as having been killed on the night of October 4 and 5. Most of these people were victims of the drunken savagery of the OMON, who used the state of emergency as an excuse to shoot with impunity at living targets, mainly people who had come from the White House.

On the following day it became possible to calculate the number of people who had been lucky—the bullets of the OMON had not killed them, and they lay in the darkness, hoping to be taken for dead. Or else, they managed to hide from the death patrols. On October 5, a total of 107 people were admitted to hospitals with gunshot wounds!

The "democrats" grouped around Yeltsin had triumphed in a difficult battle against the constitution, the law, and the representative and judicial powers. They managed also to conquer the remnants of humanity in their own souls. The democratic intelligentsia, whose members include many genuinely talented scientists, scholars, and cultural figures, called openly on October 4 and 5 for physical reprisals against their political opponents, for the illegal suppression of opposition newspapers, and for the banning—again illegally—of opposition political parties and public organizations. In this atmosphere, it is not surprising that a total contempt was shown for the victims of the bloody reprisals against supporters of the parliament. No official commission was set up to establish the number of dead and list their names, and all the efforts of a number of journalists to draw the attention of the authorities to this question have been met with silence.

Pavel Koltsov
WE FILMED IN THE MORGUE OF THE BOTKIN HOSPITAL

Nikolay Nikolayev, a camera operator with the team from the television program EKS, tells his story:

...The morgue was filled to overflowing. Corpses lay piled on stretchers, one on top of the other. Many of the corpses had horribly mutilated faces, which people had covered with towels....

An official from the prosecutor's office appeared unexpectedly, and literally flung himself at us. "Who are you? What are you doing filming here? I don't know anything about this! Turn off your cameras!"

Nevertheless, we managed to record how a closed van of the type used for transporting foodstuffs—it had several wooden compartments—drove up to the morgue, and people began gathering up corpses in plastic bags, the very bags people are still talking about, and began loading them into the van. We were naturally curious to know what van this was, and where it was going. The people brushed us aside without an answer. Someone then said that there were only sixteen or eighteen dead from the White House in the morgue, and that these corpses in plastic bags had nothing to do with the people who had been killed....

(*Nezavisimaya Gazeta,* November 10, 1993)

(The program EKS that included the video material from the morgue was taken off the air by the management of Russian Television. Later, part of this material was broadcast over the St. Petersburg television channel on the news program NTV.)

Andrey Baiduzhiy
THE VICTIMS OF THE OCTOBER EVENTS

....On the number of dead inside the White House, it can now be said confidently that the reports that hundreds or even thousands of corpses were inside the building were false. Even if we suppose that someone, somehow, managed to transport large numbers of corpses from the center of Moscow and to bury or destroy them without being observed, after a certain time the militia stations would have been flooded with appeals from relatives searching for people who had disappeared in early October....

However, the fact that some questions have been answered does not mean that all the mysteries surrounding the number of people killed in the Supreme Soviet building have been solved. Until now, we have not only lacked a final total for the number of people killed inside the White House, but the identity of some of them has not been established. The official version has it that amid the general confusion in the morgue of the ambulance research institute, the bodies of people who had been killed inside the building on the Krasnopresnenskiy Embankment were mixed with the corpses of people who had been killed near the building and also at Ostankino. As a result, establishing where particular bodies came from is now impossible....

According to statements by eyewitnesses, all forty-three of the bodies of people killed inside the White House were found on the bottom two floors. Not a single corpse was taken from the upper floors of the building, which, as is well known, came under fire from the tanks.

(*Nezavisimaya Gazeta,* November 18, 1993)

Valeriy Rogov
ANGELS WEEP OVER MOSCOW
The Victors are Silent: Neither Confirming Facts, Nor Denying Them

....This was a horrible place, like a sheep-pen—the rear walls of three administrative buildings at the Krasnaya Presnya stadium. A closed-off space of approximately forty square meters. But this was also the passageway to the swimming pool, and was paved with blue tiles. The tiles had faded by the day of remembrance.

The OMON did the shooting. The dead were dragged off to the swimming pool, a distance of twenty meters, and were thrown in there. This was stated by a woman who spent the whole night stricken with terror beneath one of the private vehicles parked opposite the pool. A woman of about fifty, in an ash-colored jacket, with a black beret on her head. Her face was emaciated, and like the jacket, ashen—from lack of sleep and emotional torment. The expression in her eyes suggested that the terror had not abated.

Two intelligent women from the building opposite related that the shooting began at dusk on October 4, and that the bloody Bacchanalia continued all night. With quavering voices, they said that whatever their views might have been prior to that day and the following night, what had happened had been monstrous, and that everyone was completely helpless before the tyranny of the authorities.

On October 7, the newspaper *Trud* remarked that it was "hard to sleep after the assault." Many of the people living near the House of Soviets were awakened "by bursts of automatic rifle fire." During the same days other newspapers—and in particular *Nezavisimaya Gazeta* on October 6—reported that as many as 600 prisoners were herded into the Krasnaya Presnya stadium, which is about a hundred meters from the House of Soviets. The victors are silent, neither confirming facts nor denying them....

Those of the prisoners who survived relate that crates of vodka—Stolichnaya, in liter bottles—had been brought to the stadium for the OMON, and that the OMON drank without restraint. The prisoners were effectively nameless; if any of them had documents, these were taken away. When selected prisoners were taken to the lower administrative buildings, they do not seem to have suspected that they were being taken off to be executed....

The Parliament building on October 7. [Photo by Vojtech Lavicka]

It is now clear that only rank-and-file defenders of the House of Soviets were shot. People, that is, whose deaths would not outrage international public opinion. Of course, the enraged victors would have preferred to start by shooting defiant deputies, opposition journalists, and anyone who was capable of putting together a coherent picture and pointing to the infernal logic of what was taking place. But they decided against this. Instead deputies, journalists, and anyone else who had shown defiance received merciless beatings.

In my view, however, the most frightening thing is that among the ruling elite there were people who demanded that no restraint be shown whatever. There were such people, and there still are.

I was shaken by the speech which the President of Kalmykiya, Kirsan Ilyumzhinov, made in Elista. Together with the President of the Ingush Republic, Ruslan Aushev, he tried to prevent a bloodbath. At 3 p.m. on October 4, Ilyumzhinov and Aushev burst into a meeting of subjects of the Russian Federation in the Kremlin. The two presidents had come directly from the White House, besieged and under fire from tank cannon. They called for mercy and reconciliation. Here I quote from the October 9 issue of the newspaper *Sovetskaya Kalmykiya*:

"To this, the Russian leaders replied that it was necessary to annihilate them completely, to wipe them from the face of the earth. Then Boris Nemtsov, the Governor of Nizhniy Novgorod, leapt in: 'Crush them, crush them, Viktor Stepanovich [Chernomyrdin, the Prime Minister of the Russian Federation—authors], there's no time left! Annihilate them!' Other regional governors as well began saying: 'Annihilate them! Shoot them all!'"

....I lit a cigarette, going over to the wire mesh of the fence. Next to me was a tall, athletic-looking young man—I would almost have said a teenager, if it weren't for the little girl about six years old, dressed in a white fur coat and looking very like him, whom he was holding tightly by the hand.

We smoked for some time, gazing silently at the wall opposite with the red stains of carnations in the bullet holes. Then, for some reason using the familiar form of address, I asked him:

"Do you know who they shot here?"

"Yes, I know," he replied firmly, giving me a searching look. "I was here that night."

"Were you one of the defenders?"

"Yes. They grabbed us on the second floor of the House of Soviets, and marched us over to the stadium." Here he fell silent.

"And...who did they shoot?"

"They shot the people who told them to their faces that the OMON were scum. Or who refused to keep their hands on their heads. They beat them up and dragged them over here.

"In general," he added in a sombre tone, "they shot everyone they didn't like. They had orders to wipe us out."

"Including you?"

"What was I worth to them?" There was a harsh shiver in his voice. "Wasn't I a commie? Wasn't I a red-brown? You know what they call us now? 'The rabble'—it's no great pity if we get wiped out."

He concluded in a muffled tone: "I survived thanks to a miracle."

(*Pravda*, December 23, 1993)

5

THE POST-OCTOBER REGIME

The political conflict of September and October 1993 had a significance extending far beyond the shelling of the Russian parliament. The conflict changed the political face of Russia, the structure of authority, and the whole temper of society.

THE DECEMBER ELECTIONS AND REFERENDUM

In order to give an appearance of legality to his coup d'état of September 21, 1993, Yeltsin decided, first, to consolidate the outcome through the adoption of a new constitution by referendum, and second, to hold the parliamentary elections that were promised for December 12. He was thus able to claim this expression of the popular will as the basis for a new system of state power. But to ensure that his opponents could not use the democratic procedures to alter the balance of forces in their favor, Yeltsin took a number of very serious steps. The nature of these steps was such that the conditions under which the elections and the referendum took place could not be called democratic.

The election campaigning took place with the main opposition newspapers either banned or suspended. The parliament's daily newspaper *Rossiyskaya Gazeta* had ceased to appear. Although some of the newspapers that had been shut down managed to have the decision reversed, this did little to alter the situation. The newspaper *Sovetskaya Rossiya* resumed publishing only a few days before the elections. Earlier, the newspaper *Pravda* had reappeared, but had then been shut down again for three weeks as a result of financial demands which the government-controlled Pressa publishing firm chose to make at precisely this moment. Meanwhile, pro-government newspapers were receiving billions of rubles in subsidies.

In the provinces, the publication of opposition newspapers was halted even though the state of emergency had been introduced only in Moscow. Local administrations locked journalists out of editorial offices, cut off access to stores of paper, and openly pressured the managers of printing works.

Strict political censorship was imposed on television broadcasts. The authorities took great pride in the fact that all the electoral blocs received an equal share of a small amount of free television time. But the political commentary in news broadcasts and in programs touching on economic and social matters had an unrelieved pro-government bias.

Aleksandr Lyubimov and Aleksandr Politkovskiy, two well-known television journalists who had begun showing independence, after initially supporting Yeltsin, and who were daring to disagree with some of the actions of the authorities, were fired. All current affairs programs on which the opposition's points of view had regularly been aired, or which had simply allowed the expression of views different from those of the authorities, were shut down. These programs included "The Parliamentary Hour," "Politburo," "Red Square," and "600 Seconds." A number of documentaries which were ready to be broadcast, but which publicized facts the authorities wanted hushed up, were not aired.

Government ministers and other high state officials belonging to pro-government electoral blocs used their administrative powers to organize their campaigns. Under threat of punishment, state employees who were subordinate to these officials gathered petition signatures for pro-government blocs and candidates. Meanwhile, top officials placed pressure on directors of enterprises and organizations that possessed meeting halls, in order to prevent supporters of opposition blocs from gathering.

The president himself set up the Central Electoral Commission. Members of regional and local electoral commissions were chosen by the Central Electoral Commission, and representatives of the opposition were not included. The presidential administration determined the provisions of the Electoral Statute and the structures of the future Federal Assembly—and revised them frequently, in some cases very substantially, while the election campaign was underway.

There were no organs to which complaints concerning arbitrary actions by the government, the presidential administration, or the Central Electoral Commission might have been addressed. The activity of the Constitutional Court had been suspended, the parliament had been bombarded, and the local organs of representative power were either dissolving themsleves on the recommendation of the President or being dissolved by decree of the President or regional administrators. In Moscow, 275 neighborhood self-management committees were shut down under an order issued by the mayor, with no reason given.

Ordinary people were powerless in the face of official lawlessness. Whether laws were obeyed, and whether legal guarantees of human rights were observed, depended solely on the good will of the authorities. The authorities, moreover, had shown their readiness to ignore all the rights of the population, even the right of peaceful citizens to stay alive; the only way ordinary people could be assured of a degree of tranquility was by demonstrating their loyalty to every official in every possible way.

Using far-fetched pretexts, electoral commissions at all levels they disallowed petition signatures collected for opposition blocs or candidates, and closed their eyes to flagrant violations committed during the collection of signatures for pro-Yeltsin blocs and candidates. The OMON raided the election headquarters of the Russian All-People's Union. As a result, petition sheets containing 25,000 signatures disappeared, and the organization's list of federal election candidates was denied registration. The Communist Party of the Russian Federation received permission to take part in the elections only two weeks before the expiration of the time allowed for petitioning. However, this did not prevent the Communist Party from outstripping almost all other parties and blocs in the number of petition signatures it submitted to register its candidates.

In setting the boundaries of the electoral districts, the Central Electoral Commission paid close attention to the results of the April 25 referendum. In regions where majorities had expressed no confidence in Yeltsin, the number of electors in each district was on average 29 percent greater than in regions that had expressed confidence in the president, even though the Electoral Statute decreed that districts could not differ in size by more than 15 percent. This particular breach gave Yeltsin supporters an advantage worth several million votes.

The text of the new constitution was also drawn up by the presidential administration, and the population was given only about a month to consider this important document before the referendum was held.

The draft constitution was intended to expand the powers of the president to the maximum possible extent. It gave the president the exclusive right to nominate candidates for Prime Minister and for the highest positions in the federal judiciary, and to appoint government ministers, high-ranking military commanders, and ambassadors personally. The procedure for removing the president from office was made so complex and difficult that a successful attempt was rendered utterly improbable.

A presidential veto on laws adopted by the Federal Assembly could be overridden only by a two-thirds majority in both houses. If the State Duma (the lower house of the Federal Assembly) were to reject three nominees for prime minister in succession, or to pass a vote of no confidence in the government, the president would be entitled to dissolve the State Duma. At the same time, the powers of the local organs of representative authority were to be sharply curtailed, and their status to be defined by the local administration.

As was to be expected, the opposition reacted extremely critically to Yeltsin's draft. Opposition leaders criticized it on television, and in a few newspapers that had re-opened. This response was met with crude denunciations and threats. The president and his aides treated any public criticism of the draft constitution or of presidential policies as unheard-of insubordination, for which the guilty parties deserved to lose their right to television time. Vice-Premier Shumeiko even sent the Central Electoral Commission a letter insisting that the Communist Party of the Russian Federation and the Democratic Party be banned from the elections, because the leaders of these parties had bitterly criticized the president and his draft constitution.

During the referendum and the elections for the Federal Assembly, no serious breaches of the electoral regulations were detected directly at the polling stations. However, the overall results gave cause for serious misgivings about the reliability of the voting figures.

The first fears arose when preliminary figures indicated that three hours before the polling stations closed, fewer than 40 per cent of electors had voted. Then immediately after voting ended, the Central Electoral Commission's total for the number of people who had taken part in the elections suddenly increased by no less than a quarter, even though all the observers testified that at the end of the day the polling stations had been practically deserted. In order for a quarter of the overall number of voters to have passed through the polling stations in the space of three hours, the stations would have had to have been much fuller toward evening than earlier in the day. This may not have been grounds for a specific accusation, but there was at least room for a puzzled enquiry.

The published results of the referendum were far more striking. According to the official figures, the sum of the people who voted for and against the draft constitution (33 million and 23.5 million, respectively) was less than the overall number of voters (58 million). Were some ballots perhaps judged invalid? There were no statements to this effect, and the reported percentages "for" and "against" (58.4% and 41.6%) added up to 100. But in this case, the absolute figures for votes "for" and "against" should also have added up to the total numbers of votes cast. What really happened? The Central Election Commission refused outright to provide explanations to journalists who sought an answer to this question.

It was not clear how the Central Electoral Commission defined the percentage of electors who took part in the voting. In the commission's official report, no figure was given for the number of registered electors. If we calculate this on the basis of the overall total of voters, we reach one figure, and if we calculate on the basis of the total votes "for" and "against," we arrive at another. Meanwhile, a third figure was cited at a press conference given by Chairperson of the Central Electoral Commission Nikolay Riabov.

According to preliminary (that is, incomplete) figures on voting in the constitutional referendum, the total of those who voted against the draft was in excess of 26 million people. Adjusted—that is, more complete—figures reduced this vote to a little over 23 million. How could this have happened? There was no answer.

Such arithmetical discrepancies in the official reports, together with the authorities' open refusal to explain or justify this situation, compelled the conclusion that the Central Electoral Commission was guilty of flagrant inaccuracy and confusion at best. Each of these inaccuracies altered the voting totals to Yeltsin's advantage. At worst, the discrepancies amounted to evidence of deliberate juggling of the voting results, carried out with complete contempt for public opinion and in confidence that no regard would be paid to protests or to demands for independent checks on the voting tallies. Whichever variant one prefers, sufficient grounds exist for asserting that the voting figures provided by the authorities were unreliable, and that the possible error amounted to millions of votes.

Even if one were to ignore the obvious facts, the draft constitution could not be considered to have been adopted for two more reasons. First, under the Referendum Law, which Yeltsin had not repealed (he had, moreover, promised to obey scrupulously all laws which did not contradict his Decree No. 1400), adopting a decision on a constitutional matter required a majority of 50 percent of registered electors. However, only about 30 percent of registered electors voted in favor of the draft. Second, and again in violation of the Referendum Law, the Central Electoral Commission refused to hold a referendum on an alternative draft constitution despite the fact that the signatures of 1,200,000 electors had been collected in the required manner on a petition in its support.

No sooner had the new constitution been proclaimed in force than Yeltsin showed he had no more respect for this document than for the old constitution on which he had recently trampled. On the first day after the new constitution came into effect, Yeltsin signed a decree on the election of new judges to the Constitutional Court. The places to be filled included those currently occupied by judges who had been legally chosen, even though the new constitution stated explicitly that the judges were to retain their powers pending the adoption of a new federal law on the Constitutional Court.

The election results, announced not long before the manuscript of this book was completed, did not bring any special surprises; under the circumstances, the outcome was predictable. The whole farce had been organized to ensure a majority for pro-Yeltsin parties. But the opposition's participation in the election campaign and its representatives' presence in the so-called Duma made it possible for even this feeble organ to serve the cause of democracy to some degree, providing a platform for public criticism of the current administration's authoritarian aspirations. The pro-Yeltsin forces proved unable to put together a stable majority.

Here, however, the authorities had allowed themselves countermoves. The new constitution allowed the dissolution of the lower house of parliament at almost any moment once it began to stand up to the president. There was no longer any need to resort to tanks and special forces troops as the main "democratic" arguments.

Also symbolic in this regard was the choice of a new name, the State Duma, for the organ of representative power. During the previous period of existence of dumas, from 1906 to 1917, these bodies had no real powers, and were dispersed by the Tsar on three occasions—each time, after the monarch decided the current duma was too talkative. The duma deputies were required to take an oath of loyalty to the Tsar. One wonders why Yeltsin did not make a similar demand of the new duma. Perhaps he does not believe any oath, having broken his own so frequently.

In any case, by the beginning of 1994, the window dressings of democracy and legitimacy had been hung up once again in Russia. The authorities were doing everything possible and impossible to ensure that the people forgot about "Bloody Monday." But it is impossible to forget this tragedy. Nor can this memory simply take the form of tributes of respect to those who died. It is important to understand the lessons of the defeat democracy, or at least democratic tendencies, suffered in Russia in October 1993.

SO WHAT HAPPENED IN RUSSIA?

Those involved in this bitter conflict represented only the pinnacle of the political elite and unusually determined activists of political parties and movements. Questions of democracy, the constitution, and the rule of law were at the center of the conflict. Although profound disagreements over economic and social policy in fact underlay the conflict, at the surface the dispute was over constitutional issues.

The main source of the contradictions dividing society was thus replaced by a secondary one—important, but nevertheless subordinate in the eyes of the majority of citizens. Here lies one of the causes of the comparatively low level of participation by ordinary citizens in the battle between Yeltsin and the parliament.

The main protagonists in the conflict were two groups within the political elite. The two sides had no fundamental strategic differences over the direction which reform in Russia ought to take. The dispute concerned only the tempo of change, the necessary social compromises, and the reordering of priorities in favor of supporting national industry. These were important disagreements, but not fundamental ones.

Precisely for this reason, Yeltsin's most active and radical opponents gave the leaders of the parliamentary side only very limited support. Even the nationalist opposition did not regard Rutskoi and Khasbulatov as dependable allies, remembering that only recently these two had been marching arm in arm with Yeltsin. The only people who allied themselves unquestioningly with Rutskoi and Khasbulatov were extremists who wanted nothing more than a pretext for acting against Yeltsin.

Meanwhile, the attempts by Rutskoi and Khasbulatov to broaden their political base by playing to the nationalist-patriotic wing of the opposition alienated a sector of the population that was ready to defend constitutional rule and democracy. It was clear that the nationalist-patriotic oppositionists had little respect for democracy and constitutional principles — no more than Yeltsin, who had carried out a coup d'état. The phrase "A plague on both your houses!" was heard frequently during the September-October crisis.

What is essential is for opposition forces that agree with the need for action within a democratic framework, and on the basis of respect for human rights, to wage an unambiguous and coordinated fight to strengthen respect for the principles of popular power. Without unity on this strategy, it will be impossible to ensure genuine mass support for efforts to restore democracy in Russia.

In the first part of our analysis, we stressed that the transitional society in Russia was objectively divided along two lines, consisting not simply of leftists (socialists) and rightists (liberals), but also of supporters of democracy and champions of the heavy hand. When the Yeltsinists who had appropriated for themselves the name of democrats finally abandoned democracy, their methods took on an increasingly authoritarian hue, and the threat of a barbarian-bureaucratic Russian variant of McCarthyism emerged. Thousands of people were then forced to recognize the need for unity between left and right in the struggle for general democratic values and human rights.

A delineation on the basis of attitudes toward democracy and human rights is emerging among supporters of both the government and the opposition. Supporters of liberal values are quitting the camp of Yeltsin, who trampled on the rule of law and carried out a bloody coup d'état. Supporters of moving toward socialism through democracy are keeping their distance from anti-Yeltsin currents that display authoritarian leanings and a contempt for human rights. It is on this basis—though not on this basis alone—that it is becoming possible to strengthen the political center, which until now has not been able to transform itself into a stable social force.

This realization has come since the early days of October, so sunny and yet so somber for us all. The first people to recognize the need for a movement to defend democracy and human rights were relatively politicized members of the democratic intelligentsia. Literally within two days of the coup a meeting took place between members of the Party of Labor, the United Social Democrats, the New Lefts, and the centrist parliamentary faction "Change/New Politics." We decided almost unanimously that a continuation of interparty wrangling was impermissible; the country needed a movement to defend democracy and human rights. We prepared an appeal, "To The Russian Public," stressing the violations of democracy and human rights by the Yeltsin administration and calling for such a movement. We also adopted a resolution, again almost unanimously, on the essentially supra-party character of the movement, and on the need to include within it broad strata of the intelligentsia, trade union and social activists, and journalists—that is, all those who until recently tried to keep themselves aloof from the dirt of national politics, but who realized after the bloody battles of October that it was impossible to stay on the sidelines any longer. The great precept of Tolstoy and Korolenko, "I cannot remain silent!" has once more become the credo of the sector of the Russian intelligentsia that is moving into activity.

This initiative group included people of very diverse ideological views. Those who had begun working together included the Marxist professor Nal Zlobin and the liberal Dmitriy Furman; they also included the dissidents and political prisoners of the Brezhnev era (and not only of that era) Petr Abovin-Egides and Gleb Pavlovskiy, the first a socialist to the marrow of his bones and the second among the founders of the Democratic Russia movement. This ideological pluralism was not artificial; it resulted from the objective need to create preconditions for Russia's transition to democracy, to create circumstances in which peaceful political and social struggles could unfold without the violation at least of a minimal set of political rights and freedoms.

The idea of the need for a social contract, an idea affirmed many years earlier by people of profoundly democratic convictions, including democratic leftists, had begun at last to open up a path for itself from below. It should be stressed that as a result of shock therapy, professors and other scholars and scientists, rank-and-file journalists, and actors had come to represent the socioeconomic, if not spiritual, lower orders of society.

Despite the open pro-Yeltsin bias of the bulk of the mass media, Russian television reported the movement's first initiatives: an October 12 press conference, and an international roundtable discussion entitled "Democracy and Elections in Russia." Admittedly, these reports were accompanied by venomous commentaries. Much more accurate information was provided by Russian radio broadcasts, including the program "Mayak" ("Beacon"); those old friends of the dissidents, Radio Liberty and the BBC; and also the politically nonaligned newspapers *Nezavisimaya Gazeta* and *Obshchaya Gazeta*, among the few relatively objective periodicals in the country.

The initiators of the movement thus managed to attract the attention of a substantial number of sympathizers, and the movement's founding conference, held only six weeks after the initiative group was formed, attracted more than 300 participants.

International solidarity was especially important for the development of our initiative. A few days after our initiative was announced, we heard of the founding in the United States of the American Committee for Democracy and Human Rights in Russia. From Spain came a memorandum of protest in the name of fifteen newspapers and public organizations, and from Greece, a letter of solidarity signed by 300 well-known public figures. In Britain a statement in defense of human rights and democracy in Russia was signed by around 100 members of the British Parliament, members of the European Parliament, and prominent trade union activists. Supporters from seven countries and the European Parliament took part in the roundtable discussion which the movement organized in Moscow a little more than two weeks after it was set up.

We have described this movement in detail not only because it is dear to us personally. An important positive lesson of the September-October coup was the practical demonstration of the fact that Russia, like the world in general, needed democracy, and that not only politicians but also large numbers of other informed citizens were ready to fight for this real and vitally important goal.

It would be wrong, however, to exaggerate the weight of the social and political currents that inscribed the words "democracy" and "human rights" on their banners. Both during the period of the September-October events and in their aftermath, the people who were actively struggling to ensure a democratic future for Russia represented only a minority of the politically active population, which itself was only a very narrow stratum.

The number of sincere defenders of democracy has turned out to be small indeed. During the period since the pro-Yeltsin forces came to power, the words "democrat" and "democracy" have come to be associated with barbaric economic experiments, with declines in living standards, with the growth of corruption and crime, and with arbitrary methods of rule. Few people have been willing to support such "democracy." Russian citizens have so far lacked the democratic traditions that would have spurred them to defend the principles of democratic government, of constitutionality, and of the rule of law. Another factor deterring people from taking part in the struggle for democracy has been the conformism implanted in them during past decades.

The problem, however, has not simply been one of traditions. In Russia, social forces that have a direct interest in the defense of democracy are almost nonexistent, or more precisely, have almost ceased to exist. In countries where bourgeois civilization holds sway, many sectors of the population have an interest in a certain level of democracy. For these sectors, democracy is an indispensable condition for a normal economic and social life. The people referred to here are usually described as the middle class, but most entrepreneurs also have an interest in democracy, as do members of the free professions and workers. For all of them, democracy signifies the conditions for regulating social conflicts, seeking compromises, ensuring necessary stability in society, and guaranteeing the rights of the individual against the possibility of tyrannical acts.

In Russia, however, most entrepreneurs are involved in criminal or semi-criminal activities, and in large-scale corruption. The reforms that have been implemented have virtually destroyed any possible basis for the existence of a middle class. Most members of the social layers that might go to make up a middle class eke out a miserable existence, forced down the social ladder to a point even lower than that of the workers. The workers have also suffered major losses during the years of reform, and have yet to see any benefits from the transition to democracy.

Nevertheless, the trade unions have clearly declared their adherence to democratic principles, if for no other reason than because it is only under conditions of democracy and constitutional rule that they have any guarantee of being able to defend the economic interests of their members. At the same time, they have been unable to play an independent political role in this conflict. The mass of trade union members have remained indifferent to political issues.

In reality, the choice the workers were offered in September and October 1993 could hardly have suited them. In most cases, they no longer trusted Yeltsin. A victory for Rutskoi and Khasbulatov, however, would not have promised them a clear change of economic policy in their favor, or firm guarantees of genuine popular power.

Meanwhile, the workers were not ready to take the helm of state administration, or even to become an influential force affecting the formulation of state policy. Russia does not possess, and has not possessed, a working class in the usual sense of the term— that is, a class of free hired workers living by the sale of their labor power. In the society of so-called real socialism, workers had the formal status of employees hired by the management of state enterprises. However, these workers were not free, since they were bound by a long series of bureaucratic restrictions. At the same time, these workers enjoyed a broad range of social welfare benefits, wider than those which hired workers usually possess.

So far, this situation has changed only to the extent that the system of social welfare is in a state of collapse. Most workers are still employed by enterprises which are not in the strict sense owned by private capital, but which are subject to a complex mix of the property rights of the higher bureaucracy, the enterprise managers, the "new rich," and in some cases, the workers themselves. The state remains corporatist in nature, and property rights are distributed on the basis of struggles and compromises between various corporations.

Consequently, a normal basis for an independent labor movement does not as yet exist in Russia, even though campaigns of economic strikes are constantly gaining strength. Workers have yet to become conscious of their distinct interests, hoping in part for a return to the paternalistic policies of the bureaucracy, and in part for private capital to voluntarily offer them a compromise. Workers lack clarity as to their political interests, although in the economic field they are already prepared to offer increasingly active resistance to the results of shock therapy policies.

Unless these facts are recognized, it will be impossible to find a basis on which the human rights defense movement, at present resting mainly on the intelligentsia, can attract the attention of broad strata of the working population—which is crucial, as long as the only organized forces in Russia are the forces of organized crime. So long as the human rights defense movement fails to address the economic, social, and cultural rights of ordinary people—even if this means avoiding any mention of socialism, and posing demands within a framework of internationally recognized rights—workers involved in the movement to defend their economic interests will not address the problem of restoring democracy.

Several possible areas of collaboration thus appear for political movements and tendencies which were formerly quite distinct. The first of these areas, providing the broadest possibilities for the unification of forces, is joint action in defense of human rights and the restoration of the democratic basis of state power. A second area is the struggle for economic and social rights, and against destructive shock therapy policies. Forces that are not entirely consistent from the point of view of the fight for democracy may link up in this struggle. Finally, there is a third area, which presupposes a more narrow collaboration. This is the unification of political forces that call for the democratic transformation of the social system on the basis of the liberation of labor—that is, of socialist tendencies.

This third area of unity is in fact a logical extension of the first two. Popular power on the political level is unattainable unless the people have corresponding power over the economy. Real political democracy is impossible without economic democracy. Such basic preconditions as political democracy and respect for human rights are necessary but not sufficient for real popular power —that is, power which extends to the economic and social fields, and not simply to politics. The advance to the economic and social power of the workers, a transition which is democratic both in form and essence, requires additional elements: the dominance of the social sector within a mixed economy, and democratic socioeconomic regulation of the economy (not just a "free" market).

These are more important and complex issues than those of democracy. But they can only be resolved under democratic conditions, once guarantees of democratic development are already in place. To the degree that social and political forces make the need to observe these conditions their starting point, they can be patriotic, socialist, or liberal-democratic, and nevertheless march side by side during the first stage of the struggle against authoritarian tendencies in Russia. The situation is the same in any other country where such a threat exists.

Unless these basic, minimal political preconditions are achieved, any struggle between leftists and rightists will proceed outside the field of democracy. It will remain no more than a clash between old and new elite groups fighting for power. In this struggle, the leftists will refer to the interests of the people, which must be defended, "naturally," by a strong state; in one way or another, this amounts to an argument for authoritarian power. The rightists refer to the need to carry out a transition to the market, which again requires the use of the heavy hand to enforce the obedience of the stupid people who fail to see the market bliss that lies before them. In both cases the people, who are supposed to be the beginning and end of any program of change, are as before left powerless and without property, even though "democracy" means "people's power."

The various unions of national-patriotic forces under the slogans of "authority" and "state power" in essence form the reverse side of the right-authoritarian tendencies of the Yeltsinists, since they rest on the effective alienation of the people from the right to decide their own fate, a right that cannot be realized outside of democracy. The ideas of the national-patriotic forces are in fact anti-popular, and thus anti-patriotic and anti-national, since both authority and the nation are secondary considerations, while human beings and their rights and freedoms are primary. An authority under which the individual human being is crushed cannot be strong. This is the lesson that must be learned from the collapse first of tsarism and the Russian Empire, and then of the USSR and the system of "real socialism."

In reality, the nationalist-statists are leading the country to the same authoritarian outcome as the Yeltsinists, even though the two sides are moving toward this point from different starting- points, and with their backs to one another.

The most important precondition for resistance to authoritarianism is the unification of democratic forces around a positive and consistently implemented program. Any attempt to forge political blocs exclusively on the basis of rejecting something or someone is doomed to failure; this fate is still more certain if the basis is personal ties between politicians or shared corporative interests. The reason is quite simple: it is impossible to resist an authoritarian-corporative authority based on behind-the-scenes deals and bureaucratic rule, and supported by the bureaucratic elite, by using methods that in essence are identical to those of the other side. As the October 1993 events confirmed, the most likely outcome of any such attempt is that the ruling clique, with its control over the state apparatus, will defeat its opponents. Even if the opposition triumphs, it will find itself taking on the role of the former authorities. To replace its severed head, the dragon of authoritarianism will grow a new one.

A union of anti-authoritarian forces, based on a program which is limited in its scope (otherwise it would not be possible to include various democratic forces), but which is substantial and concrete, and which corresponds to the interest of the majority, will prove far more durable. In Russia such a minimum program, as well as including general democratic demands (elections, the possibility of replacing office-bearers, the separation of powers, a multiparty system, guarantees of minority rights, the observance of all internationally recognized human rights, broad rights for social movements and organizations, the development of workplace and territorial self-management, and so forth) must include a minimum socioeconomic program that makes it possible to halt shock therapy.

Without such open, public unity, set out in programmatic form, the opposition has no chance of victory.

The tragic defeat of the Russian parliament fully confirmed this thesis. The constant attempts to hold behind-the-scenes discussions, and the delay in formulating an alternative program, must be rated among the key factors sealing the legislature's fate. At the same time, if the Supreme Soviet of the Russian Republic possessed any strength in the autumn of 1993, it was largely due to the fact that during the spring and summer it had gradually begun seeking to unify the opposition on the basis of general democratic demands and a socially oriented anti-crisis program for the economy. But this beginning was not pursued to its logical end.

At the critical moment, it became apparent that the Russian parliament had failed to win mass support. This clearly became the main cause of a tragic, even criminal mistake. The parliamentarians went into an alliance with extremist forces which, although in themselves not very significant, nevertheless had enough weight to cause the relationship of forces, which had been swinging in favor of the Supreme Soviet, to move back in Yeltsin's direction.

Unquestionably, one of the lessons of the October tragedy is that the political problems of anti-authoritarian struggle cannot be solved by adventurist methods or with the help of extremist forces. In our country as in any other, the real basis for democracy can only be the genuine self-organization of the people, and the support of the masses for the representative power. The Supreme Soviet of the Russian Federation was strong in that it enjoyed the support of local soviets, trade unions, and other social organizations and movements. It was weak in that the organizations supporting it were weak. Those organizations did not rest on the active participation of ordinary citizens. The trade unions could not call strikes or other decisive actions. The soviets were unable to mobilize the mass support of local residents.

The weakness of the mass base of the anti-authoritarian movement has profound causes, some of which are impossible to banish quickly—for this, long years of historical development will be required. However, the movement must not place its political stake on small, well-organized groups of political extremists, trying to make up for the inadequacies of the mass movement. Until questions of state power in Russia are no longer decided even by the army, let alone by OMON detachments from the provinces or by small groups of fighters, there will be no democracy in Russia, whichever side emerges victorious from the skirmishes.

Because the mass base of the democratic movement in Russia is so weak, there will probably be new steps along the authoritarian road. The people, tired of economic depression, chaos in public life, crime, corruption, and national conflicts, are directing their hopes toward the populist slogans of the demagogue Zhirinovsky. This shows their lack of faith in their own strength. They prefer to rely on a strong leader capable of solving their problems without their participation.

No, this is not yet the threat of fascism. Not every authoritarian regime or dictatorship which bases itself on the arbitrary exercise of power and which tramples on human rights is fascist. But in Russia, the preconditions can appear for fascism as well. When the Sturm und Drang period of nomenklatura capitalism is past; when the mass of petty traders and shady dealers who have sprung up from the normal economy and who are accustomed to quick profits are forced onto the sidelines by the implacable onset of large capital; and when the lumpenization of the working population surpasses the limits of endurance, real fascism can come to our country.

In the face of this danger, there is only one possible strategy: uniting all the forces calling for the restoration of democracy and human rights; uniting all the forces capable of throwing out the policies of shock therapy and of reviving the national economy; and uniting all the forces able to assist in the people's self-organization to struggle for their own economic, social, and political rights. As the democratic left, we see our place in the thick of this struggle, since without such a struggle there are no prospects for the socialist rebirth of our homeland.

NEWSPAPERS CITED

Solidarnost (Solidarity): a weekly newspaper published by the Moscow Federation of Trade Unions, which is closely associated with the Party of Labor.

Pravda (Truth): a daily newspaper, which in the past was subordinated to the CPSU. Now, *Pravda* is aligned with the Communist Party of the Russian Federation and other communist and socialist organisations, but maintains independence from them.

Obschaya Gazeta (Common Newspaper): a liberal intellectual weekly, which tends to be disillusioned with Yeltsin's policies, especially his violations of human rights. This newspaper was first published during the August putsch of 1991 by editors of newspapers that had been banned by the putschists. In September 1993, this newspaper began publishing on a regular basis.

Nezavisimaya Gazeta (Independent Newspaper): a daily which tries to publish a broad range of points of view (from socialist to pro-Yeltsin), but is mostly oriented to liberal opposition intellectuals.

Komsomolskaya Pravda (Komsomol Truth): a daily, formerly subordinated to the Young Communists League; now a centrist or moderate opposition newspaper.

Izvestiya (News): a strongly pro-Yeltsin newspaper, prepared by highly skilled and well-informed journalists and observers.

Moskovskie Novosti (Moscow News): a liberal intellectual weekly, centrist or moderately pro-Yeltsin. During the September and October events, *Moscow News* criticized Yeltsin from time to time from the point of view of the defense of human rights.

Segodnya (Today): a pro-Yeltsin daily. In foreign policy questions, had illusions of Russia as a great power, and therefore criticised Yeltsin's foreign policy. Directly dependent on the banking group *Most* ("Bridge.")

Trud (Labor): a centrist or moderate opposition daily, formerly the trade union newspaper, but now independent from trade unions.

Novaya Yezhednevnaya Gazeta (New Daily Newspaper): a centrist or moderate opposition newspaper created by journalists who were pushed out from pro-Yeltsin newspapers.